Advance

The Spiritual

Question Everything

"Irreverent and insightful, this is a no-nonsense guide to spirituality that can speak to the practical, the skeptical, and anyone who wants enlightenment packaged with a little fun."

—Victoria Moran, author of *Creating a Charmed Life* and *Fit from Within*

"The Spiritual Chicks come up with not only intriguing questions, but decent answers. A great coming-of-age (at any age) self-discovery manual."

—Alan Cohen, author of *Why Your Life Sucks and What You Can Do About It*

"Tami Coyne and Karen Weissman express some pretty gutsy notions about spirituality in a down-to-earth vernacular that makes it accessible to anybody."

—Emily Squires and Len Belzer, authors of *Spiritual Places In and Around New York City*

"I'm currently in the process of redefining my life after 30 years of competing on race tracks around the world—and the questions, quotes, and comments really hit home."

—Lyn St. James, 7 time Indy 500 racer, 1992 Indy 500 Rookie of the Year, and author of *Ride of Your Life*

The Spiritual Chicks
Question Everything

The Spiritual Chicks
Question Everything

Learn To Risk, Release, and Soar

Tami Coyne
and
Karen Weissman

Red Wheel
Boston, MA / York Beach, ME

First published in 2002 by
Red Wheel/Weiser, LLC
York Beach, ME
With offices at:
368 Congress Street
Boston, MA 02210
www.redwheelweiser.com

Library of Congress Cataloging-in-Publication Data

Coyne, Tami.
  The spiritual chicks question everything : learn to risk, release,
and soar / Tami Coyne and Karen Weissman.
    p. cm.
ISBN 1-59003-023-0 (pbk : alk. paper)
1. Spiritual life. 2. Women--Religious life. I. Weissman, Karen. II.
Title.
  BL625.7 .C69 2002
  248.8'43--dc21

                                                    2002006212

Typeset in Sabon
Printed in Canada
TCP

  09   08   07   06   05   04   03   02
   8   7   6   5   4   3   2   1

(For Giuseppe and Alex)

(Contents)

(PREFACE)

Who are the Spiritual Chicks and why did we write this book?

It all started in 1994 on the second floor of a brownstone in Brooklyn where every Tuesday night, without fail, a group of hardened New Yorkers gathered to discuss just how to apply spiritual principles to everyday life. One fateful night, Tami was eating a Mallomar. Karen, who had recently relocated to New York, walked into the room and exclaimed, "Hey, we never had chocolate at our metaphysics meetings in Boston!" Tami handed her a cookie and the two knew that spirituality and sugar would forever unite them.

As it turned out, we lived only a block and a half from each other, which has led to many sidewalk conversations about the nature of reality and which is the best dry cleaner in the neighborhood. Over time, we realized that while we had a lot in common and shared a similar philosophy, we approached life from opposite sides of the brain.

Tami is motivated by passion. She has paid her dues in the "real" world, working successfully in management, marketing, and recruiting, but it's really her love of music, language, and spirituality that shapes her life. Ever since childhood, singing has been her most abiding personal connection to that mysterious energy she calls Spirit, and creative self-expression has been her greatest joy. Her quest for self-knowledge has helped her understand the issues people face when trying to live authentic and creative lives and has led to her current work as a spiritually-oriented career and life coach.

Karen, on the other hand, is analytical. She has a Ph.D. in Civil Engineering and when the Chicks met, she was working as a research scientist, which, believe it or not, led her to metaphysics. The more she studied physical phenomena, the more she became convinced that the same "energy" drives everything. Her understanding of this "energy" changed her life and inspired her to teach Concept-Therapy, the metaphysically-oriented course of study where she and Tami met.

We both like to write. When we first began *The Spiritual Chicks Question Everything*, Tami had already published her first book, *Your Life's Work: A Guide to Creating a Spiritual and Successful Work Life*, and Karen thought it would be great to break the stereotype that engineers can't put a proper sentence together. Defying the myth that right-brainers and left-brainers can't connect, we became partners.

We wrote *The Spiritual Chicks Question Everything* to show that each person's life is a unique, perfectly constructed vehicle for expressing his or her spiritual nature. Real life doesn't go away when we're on the spiritual path—it *is* the spiritual path. Life isn't always easy, but when we see it as part of a bigger picture, it becomes a lot more interesting and hell of a lot more rewarding. This has certainly been true for us. We hope that this book will open up as many questions for you as it has for us.

The Spiritual Chicks

Karen Weissman & *Tami Coyne*

(ACKNOWLEDGMENTS)

The Spiritual Chicks would like to acknowledge the following people and organizations for their contributions to this book:

Arlene Weissman for her beautiful drawing;

Our editor and publisher, Robyn Heisey and Red Wheel/Weiser, Inc.;

Our agents and friends, Lisa Hagan and Sandra Martin of Paraview, Inc.;

The Concept-Therapy Institute (*www.concept-therapy.org*);

Robert Rabbin (*www.robrabbin.com*), Byron Katie (*www.thework.com*), and Carol L. Skolnick (*www.eclecticspirituality.com*) for allowing us to quote them; and

A.N. for his generosity.

(INTRODUCTION)

Despite the enduring myth that enlightenment can somehow be instantly bestowed upon us at the feet of a master, it usually takes real life to wake us up to who we are, how things actually work, and what it is we're here to do. So, let's cut to the chase. What's your real life wake-up call? Work? Relationships? An unyielding desire for the truth, inner peace, or a new car? Believe it or not, the ups and downs of everyday life are tailor made to kick us into cosmic consciousness so there's no need to sell the family farm and move to the Himalayas. In our own lives—and within each of us—is everything we need to become enlightened, which sure can be a real shock when we've been taught to rely on the experience of others rather than think for ourselves.

The Spiritual Chicks Question Everything is about using our everyday lives to gain spiritual understanding and to uncover our own power to create the lives we want to live. It doesn't matter what roles we've played over the years, how much we've struggled, or how much wisdom we've acquired up to this point. Sound intriguing? Maybe even fun? You bet it is! And it's a lot more productive than complaining about our troubles or blaming our parents, bosses, bank accounts, or international terrorists for our lack of fulfillment. It may be hard to accept at first, but it's our own beliefs that determine what we get out of life. If we don't like what we have or where we are, then it's up to us to question what we believe and throw out all the limiting ideas that keep us from being happy. It takes courage to break the chains of conventional opinion and get rid of cherished beliefs. It doesn't happen overnight. But it's well worth the effort . . . and it's a hell of a ride.

Before we get going, let's clarify a few terms. First, what exactly do we, the Spiritual Chicks, mean by "spirituality"? To us, *spirituality* is the process of exploring our connection to the universe—or, more precisely, to the elusive power that holds the entire universe together and makes our hair grow, all at the same time. OK, but what is this *power* we're talking about? Science calls it *energy* or *consciousness;* theology calls it *God* or *Spirit*. The interpretation of this power varies (scientists measure and quantify its effects, while creationists ascribe human-like body parts and personality traits to it), but there are three general characteristics that are more or less consistent: this power is everywhere, knows everything, and can do anything. Now, that's a kick-ass power. In this book, we use terms like God, energy, Spirit and consciousness, along with *Nature* and the *One Life*, interchangeably. But it's all the same ever-present stuff.

So if energy or God is everywhere, then *where* are we? And *who* are we? This brings us to the definition of the term—the *One Life Principle*—that just happens to be the foundation of this book. This ancient idea says that there is a single underlying power in the universe, but its expression takes many different forms— baseball players, puppies, exotic dancers, Supreme Court Justices, rocks, trees, even criminals. And, while you might not be ready to jump on the One Life bandwagon just yet, you must admit that this principle explains a lot about life—not the least of which is how Jerry Falwell,

Larry Flint, and Mother Theresa can all be "children of God." We're all spiritual beings, because we're all Spirit. There you have it. God, or energy, is all there is. Isn't it enlightening to realize that we've always been what we're trying to become . . . spiritual, that is?

Think about it. If we are already spiritual beings, then anything we do is spiritual whether it's praying in the highest temple or taking out the garbage. And since the One Life expresses itself through many forms, we each have our own way of exploring our spiritual connection. One person's fistfight may be as necessary for their enlightenment as another person's college education. So there's no need for spiritual name calling, labeling things as "good" or "bad." The only thing we need to consider is: Will this belief, action, idea, or conversation bring us what we say we want? The spiritual process is about questioning everything— examining every idea or concept we have to make sure that it is logical to us and that it works for us. But the trick is not to condemn anything in the process. Everything is spiritual—even stuff we don't like or don't agree with. So, we need to question everything, condemn nothing, and then align ourselves with what we want. If we can manage these three steps, we will find that our personal power is the power of the universe, and life can be pretty great.

This book offers a series of questions to help break down old, limiting beliefs, build new, more productive ideas based on the One Life Principle, and play with these new ideas so that we really learn how to use them. Along the way, we've included personal essays to show how we uncover, struggle with, and are gradually mastering this new sense of power in our own lives. So now, without further ado, here are sixty questions to rock your world.

Arlene Weissman, 2000

Part 1

Shattering the Myths

There are many myths about how to be spiritual, and most of us have bought into at least a few of them—even if we're not aware of it. These myths result in misguided beliefs about who we should be and how we should behave. They hold us back from contacting our spiritual nature—from the very source of our power to create the lives we want to live. To see things from a new perspective, we have to be willing to suspend, at least temporarily, our old beliefs. These first fifteen questions and answers reveal the most common spiritual myths and offer an alternative viewpoint.

Question 1

Do I need to go to church (synagogue, mosque, or a mountain top)?

A rubber squeeze toy in the shape of a Buddha working on a laptop computer sits in our office. The Buddha smiles complacently, from his familiar erect, yet relaxed, position that allows the proper flow of *chi* through the body. He just happens to be surfing the Web or checking his stock portfolio. Some might call this an example of the modern world "corrupting" our spiritual existence, but we think it's just the opposite. Spirituality is not something to strive for only in church, synagogue, or meditation, even though these can be useful tools. Working at the computer, mowing the lawn, or making love are also valid spiritual activities. Spirituality is not beyond real life; it *is* real life. The working Buddha reminds us of this, and that's why we keep him.

Question 2

I have a hard time meditating; can I still be spiritual?

Meditation is usually misunderstood. Most people think they have to sit in lotus position for hours every day to get anywhere. Not so. Meditation is not a technique—it is simply the state of being completely alive each and every moment. Most of the time we run on automatic pilot. We go through the motions of our lives as if we're sleepwalking. We confuse the inane chatter inside our heads for objective reasoning and seldom, if ever, experience the reality that exists outside the closed loop of our own thoughts. Did you ever notice, for instance, that when something unexpected happens, even if it's frightening, you feel the most alive and seem to act decisively, in the moment? That's because at those moments, you temporarily stop *thinking* about life and truly experience it instead. The key to achieving this state is by not removing ourselves from our daily lives, but by experiencing our surroundings with a minimum of emotional interpretation from our past memories or future worries. Each time we acknowledge a thought and let it go without analyzing it, we train ourselves to be guided by instinct and perception. These faculties put us in touch with the universal power within. And that's what meditation is all about.

A PAGE FROM LIFE

THERE'S MORE THAN ONE WAY TO FEEL YOUR POWER

I sit and try to quiet my mind, but thoughts of things I should be doing, things I need to figure out, things that interest me rush into my head. I was taught to think, to analyze, and all this analytical responsibility makes it hard for me to trust that things will work out unless I fully understand a situation beforehand. Control is important to me—I have trouble meditating, because meditation is all about letting go.

This personal trait used to trouble me. How could I be spiritual if I couldn't stop thinking long enough to get in touch with the "real me?" I tried to train myself to meditate by staring at a white sheet of paper, using a stopwatch to time how long I could keep any thoughts from entering my head. This might sound pretty anal, but I assure you that I didn't come up with this idea on my own. Anyhow, it didn't work for me. Thoughts of white sheets of paper never left my head and I couldn't stop wondering how much time had gone by. Clearing my mind was just too difficult, so I reconsidered my approach. Since I am a thinker by nature, I decided that maybe it's best not to try to cut off all thinking. Instead, I allowed myself to think about only one thing— something neutral, like a tree. When my mind wandered, I didn't press the stopwatch, I just returned to focus on the tree. I traced its trunk and all its roots in my mind. I pictured the leaves on its branches, the height of the tree, the girth of its trunk, the texture of its bark. I imagined it extracting food from the soil and assimilating the nutrients. Before I knew it, I was completely absorbed by all aspects of this mighty maple.

But this was more than just a mental distraction; I actually "merged" with the tree, for lack of a better word. It sounds cliché, becoming "one with nature," but it really was pretty cool, and not that weird or far out. In fact, it wasn't that different from the feeling I get when I'm really into a project, or having a good time. I just somehow had this idea that a truly "spiritual" occurrence had to be something far more mysterious than that.

After that experience, I realized that I don't have to ponder nothingness to know that I am part of something, that I *am* something. I am a thinker—a doer—and who's to say that that's not a spiritual mode? I feel my power by doing, by concentrating instead of meditating, by focusing my energy on one idea until I believe it strongly enough to make it a reality.

The great duality of life is that we are all basically the same natural beings, part of the same great life force.

Yet it's this common life force that also allows us our individual expression as it flows through each of us in a unique way. This duality offers us the opportunity to feel our power in two different ways, by relaxing into it in a meditative state or by using it creatively in an active state. Meditation and concentration are two sides of the same coin. Yet concentration is not given as much attention. It's considered a more earthly tool, something you use to finish your homework rather than to experience nirvana. But when I focus my mental energy to learn calculus, I'm contacting the very same power as others do when they meditate. When I remember this, I don't struggle to reach nirvana, because I know that I am already there.

Karen

For I, the LORD, your God,
am a jealous God, inflicting punishment
for their fathers' wickedness on the
children of those who hate me, down
to the third and fourth generation; but
bestowing mercy down to the thousandth
generation, on the children of those who
love me and keep my commandments.
EXODUS 20: 5-6,
The New American Bible

question 3

Will God love me
if I'm too fat?

Most of us fall into the trap of thinking that God is something or someone separate from us whose job is to judge our actions and mete out harsh punishments for our mistakes and imperfections. We pay lip service to the notion that God is within, that God is all, but inside we harbor a secret fear that a Being with a bad attitude—someone like Arnold Schwarzenegger in *The Terminator*—really exists. Our rational minds tell us this can't be so, but it can be hard to let go of old beliefs and ideas, especially when we feel imperfect and unlovable and don't know what to do about it. Snap out of it! Our feelings of "imperfection" and "unloveableness" come from worshiping false gods like *Vogue Magazine* and *The Wall Street Journal*. There is no way around it. The only way to feel God's love is to love ourselves. Forget what we're supposed to look like and how much money we're supposed to earn! When we accept our own unique perfection, we take back control over our own lives. God is the power of life in action—more like Arnold in *Terminator 2*—designed to give us what we want, without judgment. *Hasta la vista,* baby.

If the world were perfect, it wouldn't be.
YOGI BERRA

Question 4

Am I smart enough to be enlightened?

Life can seem so complicated—sometimes we wonder if we'll ever understand it. But when it comes to seeking enlightenment, intelligence is overrated. It's our minds that typically make things so complicated in the first place. We are all spiritual beings, plain and simple, and we operate with spiritual power whether we realize it or not. We can theorize about the workings of the universe, delve into the psychology of the human brain, or dissect and study the human body. But we shouldn't confuse these intellectual pursuits with the spiritual quest. There is an ancient Buddhist proverb that says, "When the student is ready, the master will appear." In other words, since there is only One Life, we implicitly have access to all the knowledge there is, so all we have to do is be ready to receive it. What makes a willing student is not whether we have barely finished high school, or whether we have a doctorate from Oxford, but rather, whether we have an earnest desire to know who we are in relation to the world around us. Whatever abilities we possess are the abilities we need to explore our higher natures. And, be assured that an earnest attempt to do so will attract helpers along the way in the form of friends, mentors, healers, or even nasty waitresses and obnoxious political pundits, who will complement our abilities, fill in the gaps, and teach us what we need to know.

A PAGE FROM LIFE

GIFTED AND TALENTED

My sister-in-law Jo Ann's umbilical cord was wrapped around her neck when she was born and the lack of oxygen damaged her brain and impaired her development. But in many ways, she's like the rest of us. Jo Ann is a beautiful woman who adores clothes and jewelry. She has a good sense of humor and loves comedies. She works at a job she sometimes likes and other times hates. In other ways, though, she's different. Jo Ann can speak both English and Italian, but she can't read or write. She'll never live on her own, and probably won't marry or have children. But she's gifted and talented. No, she can't play Chopin on the piano or recite the answers to complex math problems. Her gift is her ability to love unconditionally. Her talent is that she lets it show.

I don't mean this in some clichéd, Hallmark-sponsored-movie-of-the-week way. Jo Ann is a real person and can drive you crazy. Because her coordination isn't the best, I was left bruised after what seemed like an eternity of trying to teach her the Electric Slide on the dance floor at a family function. Jo Ann loves to take photos, but her impaired visual perception prevents her from centering her subjects in the frame. She's loud, has a temper, doesn't shake off mistreatment very easily, and has a way with foul language, which she uses to drive her feelings home just in case anyone in her vicinity hasn't figured out what she thinks. Come to think of it, she's a lot like me.

Jo Ann immediately accepted me into the family and became my friend—no questions asked. She never doubts her instincts, because she can't. If Jo Ann likes you, she likes you, end of story. She doesn't waste time analyzing problems or people. She acts completely out of feeling. Once I made the mistake of complaining about my husband in her presence. She looked at me and simply said, "He's my brother." I was humbled and promptly shut up. Relationships are everything to her. When she first met my dad, she showed him pictures of her late father and told him stories about him. She didn't ask permission to drag out the photo albums. She's not a people pleaser. She does what she wants to do. It wouldn't cross her mind to be any other way.

Jo Ann has no conception of time and neither does my husband. It must be the Italian in them. On top of her Latin nature, time has no meaning for Jo Ann because she doesn't think in a linear manner. To Jo Ann, yesterday is as good as today and last week may as well be tomorrow. Yet she remembers every single time her cousin's husband, Nicola, helped her into the water at the beach in Italy and she still talks about when my husband went to visit her at work, several years ago, and left her a big tip. I doubt that Jo Ann could tell you how old my daughter Sophia is, but she remembers her christening like it was yesterday, because she is Sophia's Godmother.

In our overachieving, perfection-oriented world, Jo Ann is perceived as a burden, an accident, a mistake of nature. But how could she be? Only a highly evolved being would choose to experience this dimension without the barrier and buffer of the mind. Only a bodhisattva could incarnate as pure love. I've seen God. She's a brain-injured Italian beauty who lives in Brooklyn.

Tami

Question 5

Do I have to give up my toys to be a spiritual person?

Let's get this straight, spirituality does not mean deprivation, in fact, it means infinite abundance. So those of us who don't want to risk sacrificing our success in the name of spiritual growth can breathe a sigh of relief. Now consider this: If something was abundant, would we hoard it? Would we stockpile it and guard it with our lives as if we were never going to see it again? If we truly believed something was abundant, we wouldn't be afraid of losing it, we'd share it with all of our friends and happily receive it from others without feeling guilty.

When we approach life with the attitude of "what can I get out of this," we draw exploitative people and situations to us. We may accumulate a lot of toys, but we'll never have peace of mind, we'll always be afraid that the toys could be taken away. Spirituality is not a consolation prize for living a life devoid of material gain. It is a mindset that allows us to actively participate in life and realize that we have access to everything we need. Be kind, be generous. We may get what we want before we even ask for it.

A PAGE FROM LIFE

MEMORANDUM

From: The Spiritual Chicks
To: Santa
RE: Revised Holiday List

Please note the following changes to our original list. We apologize for any inconvenience this may cause you.

1. ~~Matching Dolce & Gabbana wardrobes for television & mall appearances~~ Anything not manufactured in a third world sweatshop.
2. ~~Professional espresso machine for office~~ Stability in Central America
3. ~~Diamond studded watches~~ Overcoming obsession with time
4. ~~Corporate apartment in Paris~~ Housing for the homeless
5. ~~Private jet~~ Opportunities to experience other cultures
6. ~~A regular table at Nobu~~ World peace

7. ~~Personal trainers~~ We didn't really want to work this hard anyway
8. Mercedes with driver for the city and Maserati without driver, for the open road
(We've got to get around somehow—don't we?)

Question 6

I have so much to do, how can I make time to be spiritual?

What makes us think that we have to make time to "be spiritual?" God or energy is everywhere, so nothing we do is outside the realm of this universal power. If electrons, cells, and neurons gathered together in such a way as to enable us to think a certain thought, or perform a certain act, then isn't that thought or act implicitly ordained by Nature? We don't have to change what we're doing to be spiritual; we only need to observe how our actions affect us and those around us. We're not talking about overanalyzing every move. But, if a job makes you feel good, happy, or productive, then enjoy it, and if a thought or obligation makes you feel scared, jealous, or annoyed, then isn't it worth maximizing your time by trying something different in the moment to see what happens?

Spirituality is the awareness that we are connected to Life with a capital "L." This state of being is not dependent on the particular activity we are performing. So instead of denying your spiritual side until you have time to explore it, try doing what you're doing with the attitude that you already are a spiritual being, and see how your daily life is influenced as a result. If we already are spiritual, then we don't have to beat ourselves up over not trying harder, or overdoing the "wrong" thing, but at the same time, if we are connected to all of Life, then that's a pretty good reason to do the best we can at everything we do. If you have some time to sit quietly and contemplate spiritual ideals, then go for it. But everyone's life is a spiritual journey—we couldn't possibly be any less spiritual by just living.

Question 7

Do I need a guru?

Yes and no, depending on what you mean by "Guru." "Guru" literally means teacher, and yes, teachers can be helpful on the spiritual path. Swamis, lamas, Zen masters, shamans, priests, priestesses, rabbis, ministers and university professors can provide us with interesting information. But so can the ocean, the stars, the wind, mountains, children, animals, your family, your friends, and your enemies. Caught up as we are with external reality, we look for our teachers somewhere out there—and we don't need to. According to the One Life Principle, the universe is a giant mirror so all we see are our own reflections anyway. We have forgotten that we can trust our own counsel because we are spiritual beings in physical form. Call it what you will—soul, spirit, or higher self—it's in there waiting to be acknowledged and put to work. Sure, it might seem easier to follow someone who has written a bestseller, channels an extraterrestrial entity, or has a foreign accent and highly developed psychic skills, but it's the long way home. Sooner or later we have to drop the false notion that wisdom must be imparted from someone else, and learn to draw from the well of our own experience. Then, and only then, will we be in a position to see things as they really are.

A PAGE FROM LIFE

BEING HUMAN

I recently saw an episode of the TV show *Frasier*. In this episode, Frasier shows up at his friend Roz's apartment to find his psychiatrist mentor in bed with her, wearing a borrowed pink bathrobe. After that, Frasier cannot look at his mentor without seeing him in the pink satin frock that barely covers his bottom. All kidding aside, this got me thinking about the various times I caught teachers or mentors acting in ways that were contrary to my image of them. A doctor with a hacking cough, an ethics professor dating his students, a yoga instructor squealing over a spider and squashing it as if it didn't deserve the life force that was running through it. I saw a bunch of students from the massage institute near my house taking a smoking break outside. I know it's judgmental, but this bothered me. I thought massage therapists were holistic people—how can I take health advice from someone who does not take care of themselves? And in the spirituality field—boy, that's a let-down waiting to happen. The cosmically conscious are supposed to be the perfect expressions of the divine that I don't have the discipline to be, but vain gurus and the arrogant enlightened are everywhere.

Then I started to consider my own experience. I write about spirituality and teach metaphysics, but the conflicts of arranging seminars and negotiating contracts don't automatically disappear just because the subject matter is enlightenment. Human perfection (my own or anyone else's) is an oxymoron. Yet I was trying to see the perfection of the divine through the lens of imperfect human experience. Am I fit to judge perfection? Is my finite human mind capable of understanding the infinite? Who knows, maybe when we die it's the cigarette-smoking massage therapists who get into heaven first. If truth be told, it was my cloud of criticism that was keeping me from seeing the bits of perfection and goodness that are evident everywhere in human existence. And I know very well from all my studying that there would be nothing for me to criticize if I didn't recognize some of my own imperfection in the flaws of others. Having confused the teacher with the teaching, I set up a barrier that prevented me from making the teaching my own. I don't deny that we learn by example, and I try to follow the example of those who seem to know what they are doing. But if a message is true, valuable and worthy, then I can utilize this information even if it is delivered by prisoner #4528 on cellblock B. So, as always, it comes down to me—an awesome responsibility at times, but quite a relief to know that my faith can never be invalidated by the actions of another.

Karen

He who is in evil,
is also in the punishment of evil.
EMANUEL SWEDENBORG

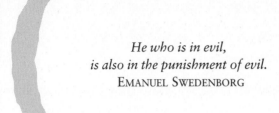

Am I doomed because of bad karma?

A few months ago, Virginia, from Peekskill, New York, wrote to us and asked, "Is there such a thing as karma? My mother said that if I don't clean my room and do my homework, I'm going to come back as an ant in my next life." We replied, "Yes, Virginia, there is such a thing as karma, although an unclean room and uncompleted homework probably won't land you ant status. Mothers can be very funny when they're tired or fed up. Ask her again after you've cleaned and studied. I bet she'll give you an upgrade."

All joking aside, Virginia is not the only one who doesn't understand karma. Most people assume it's about whether we were the Boston Strangler or St. Francis of

Assisi in a past life, whereas karma is simply the ever-present law of cause and effect that governs all aspects of creation. And, while there's no sure fire way to prove whether we reincarnate or not, most of us, at least intuitively, accept Jesus' explanation of karma, "As you sow, so shall you reap." While our victim-oriented— "it's everyone else's fault but mine"—culture probably wouldn't agree, the law of karma says that what we put into life, we get out of it. If we put a lot of hate, anger, and mistrust into life, without a doubt, we'll get the same back, not in the next life, but as a direct response to our thoughts and actions in the moment. So if we want to change our "karma," we need to forget about the past and think about what we're doing today. Now we have a really good reason to "do the right thing" because life will respond in kind. In other words, payback's a bitch—only when you act like one.

Good and Bad are not absolute.
THE KYBALION

Question 9

I'm a good person, so why do I have so much trouble getting what I want?

Believe it or not, it's not how good we are that determines what we get in life. "Good" is a relative term anyway. Ten-to-one if we're spending most of our time trying to be a saint, we're probably just playing it safe. As difficult as it can be to accept, keeping everyone else happy at the expense of our own well being is not the recipe for a fulfilling life, and here's the real shocker— it's not "spiritual." The spiritual path leads to freedom, not to never-ending obligation and compliance. It goes without saying that we should treat other people fairly, and with love and compassion. But shouldn't we also treat ourselves the same way? Being overly good is a trap that puts us in long-term martyr mode. And we all know that game too well. It's time to break free of the people-pleasing routine, and do what we really want to do. Other people might not like it at first, but they'll get over it. Hey, they might even start doing what they really want to do too. Now that's spiritual.

A PAGE FROM LIFE

THE BLAME GAME

Most of us are so good at playing the martyr role that it seems to be impossible to take complete responsibility for our own lives, no matter how hard we try. I'm not talking from a proverbial mountaintop here. I've studied spirituality for a long time and am, in fact, a card-carrying member of the "you create your own reality" school of thought. I've had some "peak" moments along the path and I know that there is one underlying essence in the universe. I've even written a book that explains how the whole thing works. And still, more often than I care to admit, I blame external circumstances and other people when things don't go my way.

Here's a recent example. I have a teleconference with a client every Sunday morning. My husband and daughter have to be up, dressed, and out of the apartment by 10:00 A.M. so that I can do my work (which I love). It used to be that my husband would take my daughter to the diner for breakfast and they would spend a few hours together while I had my phone call and got caught up on other work.

For no apparent reason, a few months ago, I decided that as part of my motherly/wifely duties, I should fix everyone a special Sunday morning breakfast before the day's activities got under way. This has created nothing but problems because there isn't enough time to get everything done in an unhurried, pleasant way. But, instead of going back to our original routine, I've stuck to the new schedule and blamed my "uncooperative" husband and child for my stress level. Why? Because I have a martyr complex, which means that I have to be the one who's working the hardest, (under the most difficult conditions) at all times. Actually, I just couldn't tolerate the lack of stress, perhaps the biggest symptom of the victim/martyr syndrome. I resisted this realization for a long time, but, to be honest, it just isn't that much fun blaming people any more. I guess I may be outgrowing my need to be a martyr. Next Sunday, I'm going to smile, be happy, and not make breakfast— even if it kills me.

Tami

question 10

Do I have to keep kosher/take vitamins/eat fish on Friday?

Human beings love ritual. We think that it's a wonderful way to feel connected to something greater than ourselves—to God, other people, or some ideal such as perfect health. But, in a way, rituals are simply a form of magical thinking designed by the mind to keep existential fear and dread at bay, and to foster a sense of superiority over others. We think that if we can just eat low fat, no fat, or fat killed a certain way, we can protect ourselves from harm. But "bad" things still happen. Airplanes crash, the economy falters, someone in our family gets sick. Still, rituals serve to draw us closer together, don't they? Performing certain rites on a regular basis and adhering to tradition no doubt can bring us closer to other members of our community, but what about those people outside our circle? Isn't it hard to connect with those who we feel are doomed to remain "unenlightened" or condemned to spend eternity in hell just because they don't share our beliefs?

There's nothing inherently wrong with keeping kosher, eating fish on Friday, or meditating six hours a day, but it doesn't increase our chances to get into the kingdom of heaven or to reach nirvana—because we're already there. We're just too busy performing rituals to realize it! And, taking vitamins, exercising five hours a day/week/month/year, and avoiding butter does not necessarily result in perfect health. But, accepting that we're already perfect as we are just might start a chain reaction that *could* result in enhanced physical well-being. Our bodies and minds need rituals to feel alive. Our souls feel alive by *living*.

A PAGE FROM LIFE

CONFESSIONS OF A HEALTH FOOD SNOB

Several years ago I went to hear Morley Safer interview two of my favorite culinary celebrities, Julia Child and Jacques Pépin. At one point, Morley asked them, "What type of culinary movements don't you like?" Julia promptly replied, "Those health food nuts." Jacques and Julia are two of my favorite icons not only because they are great chefs with lively personalities, but also because they live very happy, fulfilling lives, eating great food and drinking lots of wine and champagne.

There was a time when I would not have been so appreciative of their lifestyle. In fact, I had been one of those health food nuts to which Ms. Child so unaffectionately referred. I was a vitamin-popping, lactose-intolerant, carrot-juicing snob. I did take breaks in my regime for parties and holidays, so I was not entirely without my junk food. But basically, I was quite proud that I ate "better" than most people I knew. However, I soon learned the hard way that the pearls of garlic around my neck didn't keep away all of the evil vampires.

The year after I turned twenty-five was a challenging one for me. It was my last year of graduate school. I was extremely bored with my major after studying it for five years and I was faced with choices of where to live and what to do. My true desire was to do something adventurous—like work on infrastructure planning in a developing country, or drop engineering and move into an entirely new profession, but I was afraid. Developing countries were filled with diseases—what if I caught something? How could I change careers after receiving my doctorate? How would I support myself? So I opted for a traditional research job in Boston—it wasn't exactly India, but it was a new city where I knew almost no one. This compromise unfortunately included all of the angst of living alone in a new place, without the excitement of doing something really different from what I already knew. But I was safe, so I thought, and I was able to keep up my clean diet and lifestyle. But something wasn't quite right.

My last year in school, I had had a really bad case of mono that delayed the completion of my thesis for a semester. Now, less than a year later, I came down with a fever of 106 degrees (that's not a typo) that landed me in the hospital for five days.

What the hell was wrong? My entire life was structured around being safe and healthy, and here I was—sick. People who paid far less attention to their physical condition didn't end up in the hospital, but I did. It's as if the conflict, frustration, and fear in my life sucked the health right out of me. Ironically, that fear and conflict centered on trying to protect myself. As I recovered from this mini trauma, I realized that my life was not focused on being healthy, as I had thought it was, it was focused on not getting sick, and there's a huge difference between the two. I started thinking less about what I ate and more about what made me happy. I made new friends, kept up a long distance relationship with my boyfriend (now husband), and saw that if I wanted to, I *could* survive in a new place. When I ate healthy foods or took vitamins, it was no longer out of fear, but out of a sense of care for my own well-being.

That awful hospital experience humbled me. I let go of an old idea that health was to be preserved at all costs. After all, the price I had paid for this idea was my health! The pride I took in knowing more about nutrition than the average grocery store consumer gave way to the logical conclusion that if others are happy, active, and generally getting what they want out of life, who am I to criticize what they are eating? So when Julia Child—who still travels and records television shows at eighty-five years old, and who studied culinary arts in Paris and became a household name after she was forty—tells me to put two sticks of butter into the recipe, I plan to follow her directions and enjoy the meal.

Karen

Being has this necessary peculiarity,
that its change is brought about by
nothing external to itself.
APOLLONIUS OF TYANA

Question 11

Do I need God's approval?

The people who get what they want out of life know that they are one hundred percent responsible for what happens to them, whether it's a hurricane, car accident, illness, or stroke of good luck. They know how to focus their energy on what they want, motivate themselves when things get tough, and adapt when life throws them a curve ball. They don't waste time worrying about what others think of them, seeking revenge, or judging anyone else's way of doing things. They know that—as difficult as it may be to accept on the bad days—no one stops any of us from "making it" or "getting ahead" except ourselves. This might sound harsh, but think about it. The flip side is that we don't need anyone's approval to do anything. If Nature—another name for God—didn't like risk-takers, we'd all still be single-celled organisms swimming in the primordial soup. According to traditional theology, we were all created in the image and likeness of our Creator. Well then, shouldn't we act accordingly?

We were not put on this planet to supplicate or beg for favors from some external authority. We don't have to ask anyone for approval. We have the power to direct our lives any way we choose because we are the sons and daughters of the creative power of the universe. It's time to stand up and start living the lives of our dreams.

Try this. Start with something small: order what you really want for lunch, major in a subject you love, or break with a family tradition that makes you unhappy. The key is to do something, anything, that proves that you can make decisions for yourself and live with the consequences. In time, you'll get the hang of it. You've got the Power!

*Although the world is full of suffering, it is also
full of the overcoming of it.*
HELEN KELLER

Question 12

Don't you understand—
I have REAL problems?

It's easy to be positive and have faith in the natural order of the universe when things are going well. Whether we're having fun with friends or we've just completed a successful project at work, when life is in harmony with our desires we feel alive and in control of our own destinies. What is even more amazing than this feeling of personal power, however, is how quickly it goes out the window as soon as something doesn't go our way. "My spouse gambled away all of our savings," or, worse, "my arteries are blocked and I may need surgery." "Forget about that 'spiritual crap'—this is serious!" Admittedly, it's hard to remember, or even believe that we are spiritual beings with all the knowledge of the universe at our disposal when we feel totally blindsided by a major problem. But spirituality is about contacting that creative power within. Just because there are things in our lives that we don't like, it doesn't mean that this power has abandoned us. It simply means that it's time to go inside ourselves and see how we might use our creative power to solve the problem or, if necessary, adapt to the new situation. Despite what we've come to believe, obstacles are not punishment. They represent an internal conflict that we need to work out. It is precisely when we have *real* problems that we most need to contact our spiritual nature. When we are in contact with our innermost nature, we feel less alone, we're able to learn from our struggle, and most importantly, we recognize that the same power that created the problem can also uncreate it.

Question 13

Do I need to suffer?

There's no way to sugarcoat this: It is impossible to be human and not suffer. But what does "suffer" really mean? One definition is "to feel pain or distress," as in, "I am suffering from cancer." We all resonate with that, and for good reason. Because we have bodies, we cannot avoid the experience of physical pain—our very entry into this world involved pain and discomfort for both mother and child. And, because we are emotional creatures, it is impossible to escape feeling down or blue from time to time. In the human kingdom, pain and distress simply go with the territory—but so does joy.

There is another definition of the word "suffer" that means "to experience, feel, or undergo." We all know the saying, "Everyone must suffer the consequences of their actions." We usually ascribe a negative connotation to this thanks to the Judeo-Christian notions of judgment, sin, and human imperfection. But, "suffering," as in "experiencing," does not have to lead to a negative outcome. We can equally experience wonderful results from our actions, like when we finally get that job promotion after years of dedicated work or when we are thrilled to discover that we're going to have a baby after making love with our partner. In a real sense, "to suffer" is shorthand for the law of cause and effect. When we focus all of our attention on pain and distress—either by glorifying it or avoiding it—we create more of the same. On the other hand, when we give ourselves permission to experience and feel all the aspects of life, the ups and the downs, the joys and the challenges, we accept our magnificent role as co-creator and life becomes a spiritual adventure.

A PAGE FROM LIFE

THE ROAD TO CALVARY

As well-educated citizens of the twenty-first century, we chuckle to think that "primitive" people believed their gods were real. There is mythology, we reason, a collection of imaginary stories created to make sense of the unknown, and then there is reality. Most of us, however, do not use the same reason when contemplating the tales of our own religion.

As a Catholic by tradition, I have always been confused by the contradictory nature of the Christ story as mainstream religion presents it. On one hand, I've been deeply inspired by Jesus' dedication to the Truth and his determination to "do the right thing" despite the consequences. On the other hand, Jesus' example didn't strike me as a particularly practical way to live because of the intense suffering involved. It's not easy to get psyched about walking in Christ's footsteps if getting nailed to a cross is the big reward that waits at the end of the road. Let's be honest, when taken literally, the story itself is enough to scare the bejesus out of anyone! Who in his or her right mind would consciously choose to go against conventional wisdom and the established social order, only to end up being tortured and killed? For most of us, the improbable promise of supernatural resurrection doesn't do much to sweeten the deal.

The way that nearly every Christian church in the world depicts Christ—nailed to the cross on the verge of death—does not stimulate the desire for spiritual transcendence in the hearts of most people. Even if we're unaware of it, this gruesome image comes across more like a warning about what happens to those who preach a version of the truth that is in opposition to accepted dogma. At the very least, it is an effective, graphic advertisement for pain and suffering. The two cornerstones of Christianity—the concept of "original sin" (which was not even one of Jesus' own teachings) and the idea that Jesus died for our sins—emphasize pain and suffering as the human condition. Not only that, they don't make good philosophical sense. Even before the story of Adam and Eve's downfall, which is the root of original sin, God says, "Let us make man in our image, after our likeness . . . "(Gen 1: 26). Now, if we're made in the image of our Creator, who we accept is all present, all powerful, and all knowing, how can we be born in sin unless God is sinful, which clearly goes against the accepted attributes of the Creator? If God is everywhere, knows everything, and has all the power, how can sin exist? And if there isn't any such thing as sin, just what was Jesus doing up there on that cross?

In addition to the horrifying nature of the story itself and the philosophical inconsistencies within the Christian tradition, there is the unthinkable question as to whether a man called Jesus ever lived at all. Some reputable scholars challenge the idea that Jesus was a living human being born on December 25 to the Virgin Mary. The field of comparative religion has shown striking similarities between the Christ story, the Osiris/ Dionysus myth, the accounts of Buddha and Krishna, and the life of Apollonius of Tyana. As a result, more and more people are seeing the Christ story as a myth, an allegory, or a symbolic representation of the universal journey to spiritual realization or at-one-ment with God.

Despite my life long quest for spiritual under-standing, I have only recently had the courage to question the historical existence of Jesus Christ. I'm a logical person, was encouraged since early childhood to question things that didn't make sense to me, and wasn't even very well trained in my own religion. So why exactly is the idea that Jesus is a myth such a rad-ical notion? Because the message of the Christ story itself says that going against the norm is serious busi-ness. Even highly educated people will not risk the threat of eternal damnation and hellfire to question the "mysteries of the church." But letting go of the official interpretation of the life of Jesus Christ is the only way to discover the Christ within—which really seems to be what Jesus was saying—that everything from the kingdom of heaven to the power to heal is within us, just as it was within him. Once we realize that the crucifixion was not about pain and suffering, but about freedom, we might be able to believe in resurrection—not the supernatural variety, but a new life in Spirit, liberated from the incessant demands of the ego and material reality. If we can begin to uncover the Truth of the Jesus myth for ourselves, we might come to see that not only are we all on the road to Calvary, but that there's no reason we can't enjoy the trip.

Tami

*In every human being is the imprint
of all that has gone before, especially
the imprint of his direct ancestors. And
not only that, but that it is the imprint of
all the environment in which he has lived,
and that human responsibility is utterly
unscientific, and besides that, horribly cruel.*
CLARENCE DARROW

Question 14

If I have free will,
how come I keep making
the same mistakes?

We say to ourselves, "The next time she criticizes me,
I'm not going to get upset." But before we know it, we fly
off the handle with defensiveness. We swear to stop dating
bossy jerks, but repeat the same old pattern again and
again. Are some people just destined to make bad choices?
Well, yes and no. Free will is a funky concept. On the
one hand, we have a brain that allows us to analyze a
situation and act accordingly. However, our brain can
only work with the raw data that has been entered into
it—through education, ancestry, and our own life
experience. If deep down we are insecure, it's going to
be hard to ignore a critical person or have the confidence
to tell them off. So, in some sense it is our destiny to

suffer through these types of experiences until we learn to conquer them. Hence, the over-used, not-so-comforting, but nonetheless true expression "everything happens for a reason." Free will evolves as we evolve. It's too damn hard to fight those feelings of anger in the middle of a situation that really pisses us off. However, if we deliberately seek out experiences where we can be patient, understanding, and forgiving, then we will have some data to draw on the next time we are confronted with a volatile situation. Let's use free will to change our nature, and let destiny play out the rest.

Man is but a shadow of a dream.
PINDAR, PYTHIAN ODES 8, FIFTH CENTURY B.C.

Question 15

Do I have to go it alone?

Does it seem like a lonely road doing what you believe, following your heart, trusting your instincts? Yeah, it can seem that way. And, when it comes down to it, no one but you can determine the right course of action for your life and spiritual growth. But the point most often overlooked is that conflict, lack of support, and even loneliness are actually the result of not following our own paths. It's like when you're a kid in Junior High trying so hard to fit in with the crowd, but your efforts to conform only reinforce how different you feel. Then, one summer, you finally admit that you really are more interested in science than in shopping or in football, and your parents send you to space camp. You meet all sorts of great people there who you connect with just by being yourself.

When we are true to ourselves, there may be some people who don't understand us, but we will always find others who will help us along in life. While it's nice to be appreciated by others, deep down, we know the difference between being appreciated for something meaningful to us and something superficial, or worse yet, contrary to us. Who needs support for something we don't want to do in the first place? Be bold, be brave, be yourself. You may find you're all the company you need.

A PAGE FROM LIFE

ME AND VINCENT VAN GOGH

"I don't get enough support" has been my mantra for most of my life. But, the kicker is that it's not really true. It's simply an excerpt from the on-going interior monologue written, directed, and produced by my ego for my ego. We all tell ourselves stories, yet we rarely stop to think about where they come from or how they affect, or should I say direct, our lives.

My particular story comes from having a contradictory nature. I'm a born risk taker with strong people-pleasing tendencies. In other words, I love going where others fear to tread, but I want a cheerleading squad to accompany me every step of the way. Needless to say, this is not how risk taking works. Don't misunderstand me, I have no desire to drive a race car or become an Olympic skier. Physical risks are not my forte—just ask my husband to describe the look on my face when the car goes over sixty miles per hour or I'm careening down the bunny slope at a speed most pre-schoolers could beat on a bad day. I do, however, enjoy sailing in the uncharted waters of the soul, and find myself compelled to follow my heart, even when a successful outcome seems to be a long shot. I'm an intuitive and an empathetic person and find it easy to read people and perceive the subtext in most situations. As a result, I know what to say and when to say it, and am very good at pleasing others and giving emotional support. Strangely enough, however, despite my sensitivity to others, I've assumed that everyone enjoys forging new paths and is just as intuitive and empathetic as I am. This mis-perception has caused me a lot of unnecessary pain and heartache.

The turning point in my life came one day during a teary psychotherapy session when I was in my late-twenties. I was telling my therapist about some incident that proved how misunderstood and badly treated I had been in some meaningless situation when she said, "I understand how you must feel, Tami, but not everyone is like you." I was stunned by the implications of this simple and obviously true statement. Maybe people weren't going out of their way to hurt me. Perhaps they weren't deliberately being unsupportive, they simply weren't on my wavelength and didn't know what to say to comfort me. I realized that I had to stop taking myself so seriously and other people so personally. I could either go through life feeling as misunderstood as Vincent Van Gogh without the artistic brilliance to back it up, or stop seeking affirmation and start taking some risks that I really wanted to take.

Support is a tricky thing. We all need it, but most of us aren't very good at giving it to ourselves. We think validation has to come from external sources—from our parents, friends, teachers, or bosses. But external reality does not exist except as a reflection of our beliefs. When I'm not receiving support, it is because I am not giving myself support, plain and simple. It's not always easy for me to accept the reality of my role as the creator of my experience, but that doesn't mean it's not true. I'm much happier since I realized that, in a very real way, I am alone—and that being alone is a good thing because I don't need to waste my time waiting for support from anyone else. Now, when I feel like I need some support, I think about what I would tell someone else in a similar position and I talk to myself until I feel better. Sometimes it takes days, but it works. I'm no hero, though. When I'm really stressed out, I still catch myself repeating my old mantra, "I don't get enough support." But now I know it's a lie and I laugh.

Tami

Arlene Weissman, 2000

PART 2

Down and Dirty Practical Maneuvers

Simply suspending old beliefs won't cut it for long; we need some practical experience to back up our new perspective on what it means to be spiritual in relation to the One Life Principle. Part 2 is a field guide to help you gain experience in the real world. It contains experiments, exercises, and essays designed to show that:

1. reality is more malleable than we think,
2. we have more control over what happens to us than we realize, and
3. what we focus on, or give our energy to, determines what we get in life.

Happiness is when what you think, what you say, and what you do are in harmony.
MAHATMA GANDHI

Question 16

How would you act if you were happy?

Would you:
- smile?
- do a little dance?
- be more forgiving of other people's mistakes or of your own mistakes?
- call a friend to do something fun?
- tell someone you love them?
- try something new without worrying about succeeding or failing?
- gravitate towards other happy people or lift the spirits of those around you?

- work toward what you want instead of feeling victimized by outside circumstances?
- take more enjoyment in what you have?
- feel less attached to what you possess?
- take care of yourself?
- not be concerned with what other people think of you?

Most of us have figured out that what we give is what we get back. So why haven't we already done these things? Because it's hard. Let's face it, sometimes it's just more fun being angry, and it's easier to blame anyone other than ourselves when things don't go our way. Happiness, just like anger, is a choice. Next time you're angry, do a little dance and see what happens.

Question 17

Does "positive" thinking really work?

Positive thinking alone will not get you what you want. You must also speak positively, act positively, and, most importantly, you must believe that it is *possible* to change your reality at will. Did you ever feel as if you're an actor in a play and the director forgot to give you a copy of the script? This sense of powerlessness is very common, and it stops us from getting what we want. Ironically, we actually are in control of what we experience through the law of attraction that states, "like attracts like." Want to experience first hand what this means? Pick a day when you feel like being an actor. Go the store and act testy, impatient, and irritable with everyone you meet. Notice what happens as a result. How do people respond? How does the world look?

How does your body feel? What thoughts do you have? Give yourself a little time to unwind and then go back out and be patient, kind, and loving, no matter what happens or who you meet along the way. Lip service alone won't cut it, put some verity into your performance. How do you feel now? Hire yourself as the director and the scriptwriter and create the life you want to live.

A PAGE FROM LIFE

PREPARING FOR THE BEST— A CORPORATE STRATEGY

Einstein said that it is impossible to simultaneously promote peace and prepare for war—a rather ironic point coming from someone whose work led to the development of some pretty heavy artillery. But he's right, there's no way around it. To effectively execute a task, you have to make your efforts consistent with your goal. If you want potatoes, don't plant beets. If you want peace, don't build weapons. And, if you're building weapons, don't divert your attention with some notion of voluntary goodwill, and admit that your goal is to be strong so that no one will mess with you. I'm not saying that one approach is necessarily better than the other, I'm only saying that pretending that we want one thing, while all our actions work toward another is basically counterproductive.

This hypocrisy is often found in business situations. I should know because I have been guilty of perpetuating it myself. I wanted success, yet I was too busy ferreting out potential problems to recognize many creative opportunities. I wanted a bigger staff and good relationships with my coworkers, yet I had a hard time delegating responsibility, thinking I had to be involved at every level. These are hard patterns to break, but eventually the burden of preparing for the worst wore me out and I knew I had to try something different.

Feigning a positive attitude never made much sense to me, but as I learned more about the One Life Principle, I began to understand the direct relationship between expectations and outcomes. I started to test this relationship in my dealings with my small research staff. I wanted a capable, independent staff, so I decided to treat them as if they were just that. I stopped looking over their shoulders and gave them space to do their work. The response was very interesting. Some people rose to the occasion—working independently and seeking help when they needed it. They also began to contribute their own creative ideas in a way they never would have under the old regime. One person, who had been quite comfortable with my previous micromanagement style, became quite nervous and would check in with me every five minutes. We had to work on this. Then there was the hard-core complainer. This person had always given me a lot of trouble, feeding my fears of doom and gloom. But now I was no longer indulging him. He tried to rile others in the department, but they were happy with the new arrangements and just found him annoying. His destructive nature soon became clear to everyone and at a certain point I knew he had to go. As a happy "accident," an opening came up in another department and he migrated out before I had to fire him.

This was an amazing experience. My biggest fear had been that I would be blindsided by problems if I didn't diligently try to anticipate them. Instead, by expecting the best, I ended up uncovering problems both within myself and within the organization that had kept all of us from realizing our potential. And when these were addressed, I was left with a group that was motivated and ready to achieve, rather than battle worn from having to prove themselves to me.

In a way, I was lucky that my fear was such an obvious impediment in the business world because it forced me to deal with it early on. Preparing for the best is still a conscious effort for me. At the beginning of a new venture, I often feel like I have just walked off a cliff, and occasionally, an unexpected problem comes up and I have to regroup. But with each experience, I gain more confidence in the infallible law of cause and effect which governs every aspect of our universe, and I know that to get the best out of life, I have to prepare myself to receive it.

Karen

Question 18

What's love got to do with it?

Love supposedly plays a big role in our lives. But do we really know what love is? Most often what we think of as love is a knee-jerk reaction triggered by our own fears and designed to protect our own interests. For some, these fears come from having accepted a judgmental and meddlesome God as a role model for human interaction. For others, they stem from a lack of faith in the existence of any sort of universal power—so it's every man or woman for him- or herself. We've chosen five emotional reactions that commonly pass for love to expose the truth behind the illusion. What's love got to do with it? You be the judge.

1. **I'm jealous when my lover talks to other men/ women.**

    Jealousy is often viewed as proof of love, but it really reflects a subconscious insecurity and mistrust. Jealousy stems from greed and selfishness—not love—and is about ownership. On the spiritual level, we are all one; therefore it is impossible to own (or control) another individual. Don't misunderstand. You don't have to put up with hurtful behavior, but when jealousy rears its ugly head, love yourself enough to get to the bottom of the issue by uncovering why you feel so insecure. Once you've figured out your part in the problem, you can determine the proper course of action. One thing is for certain, jealousy plays no role in a truly loving relationship.

2. **I'm still grieving for my parent who died several years ago.**

    Grieving is not for the dead, it's an indulgence for the living. While mourning a loved one may be psychologically necessary for a period of time, let's not add to the stress by pretending we owe it to the person who died to disrupt our lives for an extended period of time. This might seem disrespectful on the surface, but on a deeper level it shows profound respect and love for life, which includes the eventual death of the body. Love is not a physical thing, so therefore love did not die. Focusing on the positive feelings you had for the person who died, and remembering the love you shared with him or her invites more love into your life and keeps love alive eternally.

3. **My children are going to college whether they want to or not.**

    It's natural to want the best for our children, but when we impose our will on them, we run the risk of interfering with their growth and progress. True love is about encouraging your children (or anyone for that matter) to evolve in their own time, even if they make a choice you think they will regret later. If we try to make the "right" decision in spite of their wishes, often times, the only thing they will develop is resentment. Back off, bite your tongue and treat them as the wise decision makers you'd like them to be. Who knows, they might know themselves better than you think.

4. **I'm angry at my friend's decision not to undergo chemotherapy and radiation for breast cancer, and I tried to talk some sense into her.**

    While this might sound caring and responsible, telling other people how to live their lives, or even worrying about how they live their lives is about fear, not love. There's no one "right" solution, even in matters of life and death. If all you see is what your friend is *not* doing, then maybe you need to gain a deeper understanding of what she *is* doing and what she wants to achieve. The next time you find yourself about to utter the words "it's just because I care about you," stop and think if it's actually because "your way contradicts my way so it can't be any good."

5. **My spouse doesn't like to travel so I turned down a once-in-a-lifetime opportunity to visit Japan so I wouldn't leave him/her home alone.**

    Self-sacrifice is often viewed as a loving act, but it's usually unnecessary martyrdom. We all have duties to our jobs and families, and we sometimes perform less than desirable tasks lovingly because we know they will lead to greater goals. But when duty turns into self-induced oppression, it might seem like we're pleasing others, but in the long run, we end up being resentful, depleted, and of no use to anyone. It's a hard pattern to change, so start with something small—like an afternoon drive. If the earth doesn't come to a grinding halt, you may have more freedom to take that trip around the world than you realized. If there is some fallout, at least you can deal with it in small doses, one step at a time.

In this day and age, the greatest devotion, greater than learning and praying, consists in accepting the world exactly as it happens to be.
RABBI MOSHE OF KOBRYN

Question 19

Why not contact your inner vegetable?

Sometimes, for whatever reason, things don't turn out the way we like. Maybe we're confused about what we really want, or maybe there's something better waiting for us. But until we have the clarity that usually comes from hindsight, we think, "What the hell am I going to do now?" It may seem unlikely, but we've found an unexpected source of inspiration in the plant world. Most people associate vegetation with laziness or inactivity, when in reality, plants are some of the most innovative and adaptive creatures around. Trees split their trunks to grow around obstructions. Houseplants twist and turn to grow towards a single ray of light. Potatoes and onions take root in a glass of water (or even in your refrigerator).

And weeds, my God, no matter how hard they're hit, they keep coming back for more. So what does this have to do with us humans? Well, we have this ability to adapt and create new opportunities too. It even happens within our bodies. Some people with impaired vision develop keen hearing; some with brain injuries recover their memories as the brain establishes new pathways to access stored information; and in some cases of damaged reproductive systems, the fallopian tube on one side bends to receive an egg from an ovary on the other side. If that's not plant-like adaptation, what is? So, the next time you're faced with a situation that you would never have consciously wished upon yourself, try contacting your inner vegetable to help you out.

A PAGE FROM LIFE

LIFE TAKES CARE OF ITS OWN

I was excited as the Air France charter flight touched down at Orly airport. I had wanted to live and study in Paris since I was in second grade—and now, ten years later, I was about to embark on an adventure of a lifetime. I was also scared out of my mind. Because of the charter flight schedule, there was a gap of a few days between my arrival in France and my rendezvous with the other junior-year abroaders, and the prospect of spending so much time alone in a foreign city made me feel more nervous, tense, and anxious than I had ever felt before.

As much as I tried, I couldn't control the thoughts swirling around in my head. Would anyone help me? How would I find my way? Would I remember how to speak French? Desperate to avoid mental collapse, I dug deep into my memory and dredged up some life experiences that showed I would probably be able to handle the situation. I had made it through the first few days of college, hadn't I? When I spoke French in Montreal people understood me, didn't they? I had never been a missing person, had I? So what was my problem? I told myself to buck up, have some faith, and adapt. I was going to France, after all, not solitary confinement in a federal penitentiary.

After I collected my luggage at the airport, a wonderful French woman, whom I had met on the flight, took a taxi with me to the city. She gave me her phone number and told me not to worry; she said I spoke French well and would be just fine. I stayed at a youth hostel on the Right Bank, and almost as soon as I arrived, I met some young American women who were also staying at the hostel. They were relieved that I spoke French and we traveled around the city for the next few days—never once getting lost. At the end of my first day, everything was going well, so I began to relax. I soon realized that I loved Paris just as much as I thought I would and that I felt strangely at home in my new environment. Eventually, I met up with the students with whom I would be spending the rest of the year and my initiation to life in France was complete. I never felt more relieved, self-confident, or alive in my whole life. By the time my junior year was over, I was a new person having gained a taste of the freedom that comes from being able to adapt. *Tami*

Question 20

What does it mean to be truthful?

Being truthful means speaking of what we *know*—
not what we *believe* or have *heard* a million times on
television. Yet knowing is based on our own experiences,
which of course can vary greatly from person to person.
This explains why things that seem obviously true to us
can be completely dismissed by someone else. The only
thing we can claim to know is ourselves, and even that
knowledge seems a bit shaky at times. Before being
truthful with others, we need to be honest with ourselves
about how our own beliefs or concepts may color the
truth. Once we're reasonably sure we know what the
truth is, we need to take care that others are ready to
hear this information—otherwise it's like telling a child

there's no Santa Claus before they're ready to give up their belief. Instead of telling other people "how it is," see if there's a way you can help them experience their truth for themselves. Sometimes this means giving examples, sometimes it means letting them go their own way, to learn their own lessons, which are the ones that really stick. If we focus on acting in a way that allows for the greatest amount of growth for everyone involved, including ourselves, then the truth will be revealed naturally, in its own time, even if we don't say a word.

*Everyone and everything
around you is your teacher.*
KEN KEYES, JR.
HANDBOOK TO HIGHER CONSCIOUSNESS

Question 21

Why are some people so hard to deal with?

Because they reflect back to us the aspects of our own personalities that we haven't yet confronted and which are holding us back from getting what we want. Don't believe it? Get a piece of paper and divide it into six columns. In column 1, write down the name of a person with whom you are experiencing difficulty. (It feels good to rat this bum out, doesn't it?) In column 2, write down any family members or other people in your life this person reminds you of. (Gee, this has been going on since childhood, hasn't it?) In column 3, identify all the negative qualities of the person in column 1. (You know, angry, confrontational, insensitive, etc.) In column 4, make a list of recent occasions when you have exhibited these same qualities. (Come on now, you know you have!) In column 5, write down what causes you to exhibit this negative behavior. (Easy does it. This might not be simple to figure out, but you can do it. . . .) In column 6, write down what steps you can take to change your negative behavior. (Wow, this is much cheaper than therapy!) Hey wait a minute! What about those people in columns 1 and 2? Put your plan from column 6 into action and you'll soon be amazed at how those nasty ole people have changed.

A PAGE FROM LIFE

VIBRATIONS

It may not seem like it, but in the physical world, everything vibrates, everything is in motion. Whether an object is hard like a bowling ball or soft like a pillow is related to specific rates of movement deep within. All matter has a vibratory character, and is, in turn, affected by outside energy of a similar vibratory nature—a phenomenon called resonance. Marching troops can collapse a footbridge with the collective energy of their synchronized footsteps; earthquakes can make solid brick buildings shake like jelly. But did you know that during the very same earthquake a modern skyscraper may stand tall, or a bamboo hut may sway easily with the earth's motion but return to normal after the tremor is over? Unlike the brick building, these structures are not in resonance with the earthquake's vibration and are relatively unaffected by it.

As a scientist, I have spent a large part of my adult life studying vibrations. I have seen proof of the physical phenomenon of resonance. And it makes sense to me that this physical principle would also apply to the world of thought, to the world of metaphysics. Just like matter, every idea or belief must have a certain rate of vibration associated with it. Each time a situation or idea comes along that is in resonance with one of our beliefs, we respond. No resonance, minimal response. This creates our world.

For example, I like stormy weather because I find it cozy to sit inside and write on a rainy day. My husband, on the other hand, doesn't because he can't ride his scooter to work in the rain. People on the street seem to go about their business as usual, almost indifferent to the fact that it's raining at all. Each of us responds to the rain according to our own makeup.

It's pretty easy to see the logic in the rain example, but I discovered that the principle of resonance goes even further. For example, I don't like nasty people. No one does—but I'm particularly sensitive and find it difficult to let rude comments roll off my back. When a neighbor I barely knew nearly bit my head off over a problem in our apartment building that wasn't my fault, I was really hurt. But, as self-righteous as I felt, the law of resonance tells me that I would not even have noticed how nasty this person was if I didn't have some degree of hate or criticism in me. What a shock that was, but after seeing how a mighty structure could be shaken *only* by the right vibration, how could I ignore the possibility that I was somehow tuned into this nasty behavior?

I decided to call my neighbor and find out why he thought that I had caused this problem. He wasn't home, and when I left a message with his wife, I found out that they had had a big fight right before he had ran into me. Had I known that at the time, I would not have taken his comments so personally. But instead of assuming that there must be some other reason for his illogical outburst, I resonated with his idea that I was somehow to blame.

Entire fields of engineering are devoted to redesigning structures so that they are no longer in resonance with unwanted energies. What I have learned from the remarkable consistency between the nature of physical matter and thought is that I can redesign my own way of thinking to resonate with the good in life. While there will always be earthquakes and tremors, I won't feel them so greatly, and then when a great opera singer sustains that special note, I'll ring in resonance with the joy of the music.

Karen

We know the truth, not only by reason,
but also by the heart.
BLAISE PASCAL

Question 22

Are you paying enough attention to your intuition?

If we accept the underlying premise of this book—that there is only One Life and we are all expressions of it—then it is logical to assume that because we aren't separate from anything, we have access to everything. And, because we're all made of the same stuff, we're all intuitive, whether we realize it or not. Alright, so intuition is real. But what is it and how can we use it?

Let's back up for a minute. There's no doubt that we live in a world of cause and effect. It rains in April and then the daffodils begin to bloom. One nation declares war on another and thousands of people die. When we really believe we're worthy of love, we find that partner for whom we've been longing. A profound understanding of this natural law leads to the inevitable conclusion that causes belong to the inner realm, while the tangible manifestations in the outer world are the effects. In the land of effects, "reason," or logic, is king, but in the inner world, where everything begins, "intuition," or direct knowing, is queen.

When we begin to deal directly with causes, rather than effects, our intuition naturally develops without any conscious effort on our part. We spontaneously understand why we've created certain situations, and how to get out of them or attract more of them, without racking our brains or reading countless self-help manuals. We don't need to seek outside counsel every time we have an issue, which saves wear and tear on friendships and cuts phone bills literally in half! The only way to learn to use your intuition is to listen to it, take its advice, and see what happens as a result. Keep in mind, however, the results are not always intended for short-term gratification. Your intuition knows everything there is to know about everything, so keep the faith. Soon you'll see just how much easier (and more fun) life can be as a spiritual being.

*There is nothing so absurd that it cannot be
believed as truth if repeated often enough.*
WILLIAM JAMES

Question 23

Where did you get that idea?

There isn't a single human being who hasn't had some experience with rumors, as either the subject or the perpetrator of dubious information. As a result, we all know too well just how easy it is to spread rumors and how hard it is to retract them. Once an idea is on everybody's lips, it seems to take on the appearance of established fact, even if it's completely unfounded. Observing this social phenomenon makes us wonder how many of the supposed "truths" in our own heads are there simply because we've heard them enough times. We like to think that we are discriminating and not so gullible, but if enough doctors and TV commercials tell us that it's flu season, will we begin to cough and sneeze?

If the news tells us that the economy is slow, will we approach our job with fear and suspicion, anticipating the worst? It's like we're hypnotized—so if someone says we're a chicken, we cluck. The power within each of us is indifferent to the ideas that we hold, and will carry them out in the physical world as best it can, regardless of whether they are true or false, helpful or destructive. So it pays to be careful about what we think, and to make sure that our beliefs stand up to the light of reason.

So judge your health by how *you* feel and not by the prevailing attitude of the season. Approach your success by putting your best foot forward, so that even if your company folds, you will be the standout candidate who is referred to another job. In other words, don't accept every suggestion that comes your way. And the next time you find yourself clucking like a chicken, ask yourself who the "Amazing Kreskin" was that gave you that idea in the first place, and then give him a metaphoric kick in the butt.

A PAGE FROM LIFE

EVERYDAY MANTRAS

People love to make fun of mantras. Just the thought of saying something positive to ourselves conjures up images of Stuart Smalley's (a.k.a. Al Franken) "I'm good enough, I'm smart enough and doggone it, people like me." Whether we realize it or not, or, should we say admit to it or not, almost all of us have mantras. But while some of them are encouraging, others are down right depressing. We did a little informal research and came up with our list of the top ten negative mantras in everyday use. Once you realize how much these little sayings influence your life, Stuart Smalley might not look so bad after all.

10. **Whatever.**—C'mon, we really do care what happens—don't we?
9. **People are no damn good!**—It may be true, but do we want to keep reinforcing it?
8. **Not again!**—Aren't we tired of being victims?
7. **Better safe than sorry.**—Better said than lived— unless we plan never to leave the house.
6. **Why does this always happen when I'm running late?**—Do we really want to be doing what we're doing if so much seems to be getting in our way?
5. **That's why they call it work!**—And we wonder why we hate our jobs.
4. **I can't take it any more.**—Are things really that bad, or are we just resisting what's happening at the moment?
3. **If it weren't for bad luck, I'd have no luck at all.**—Don't head to Vegas with this attitude.
2. **I want this so badly.**—How come no one ever says, "I want this so goodly?"
1. **Shit!**—This mantra just stinks!

The Spiritual Chicks

Don't agonize. Organize.
FLORYNCE KENNEDY

question 24

What are you organizing your life around?

Even if you think you're the most disorganized person on earth, we guarantee that you're organizing your life around something. Sometimes we're aware of what we're doing, like when we train for a marathon by running regularly, eating energy food, and lifting weights. Other times, we're motivated subconsciously, like when a rebellious teenager insists he knows what he's doing, but is actually drawn to anything that would piss off his parents. Whether our goals are lofty or unambitious, pleasing or fear-based, we structure our routines and lifestyles accordingly. Once these structures are in place, their sturdy boundaries keep us in line with our goal.

Our life structures take a while to erect, and almost as long to tear down, but we shouldn't be afraid to rebuild if we find that we unwittingly crystallized ourselves around something unattainable (an airbrushed picture of the latest supermodel that even she couldn't replicate in person), illogical ("I'll be happy when I win the lottery."), or no longer desirable to us ("I have to be engaged to be married by my senior year in college."). Organization is a powerful tool that operates on many levels—individually, in groups, and in societies. So the question is worth considering—"what are you organizing your life around?"

We do without doing and everything gets done.
RALPH BLUM
THE BOOK OF RUNES

question 25

Why do you think you need to do something?

The Spiritual Chicks approach to enlightenment is about using all the different resources available to improve our lives. Despite the prevailing belief that every situation requires some form of action, sometimes the best resource we have is our ability to wait patiently. But waiting, without feeling like we are wimping out, requires a genuine expectation that things will pick up again naturally without our intervention. We all know the obvious cycles of life—seasons, tides, birth and death— but until we've experienced enough personal ups and downs to know that even situations that completely suck will eventually pass, we tend to tear our hair out trying to work through an economic recession, a personal crisis, or even a bad hair day. Rhythm is a law of nature, and it's far better to work with the law than to fight against it. In the end, nature always wins.

So, if you're not feeling well, give your body some time to recover; if you don't have a date on Saturday night, crack open that novel you haven't had time to read and wait for the dry spell to end; and if things generally don't seem to be going your way, try letting life's pendulum swing where it may and quietly reorient yourself towards the direction you want to go. Then, when the pendulum swings back, as it always does, you'll have the weight of the law of rhythm behind you.

A PAGE FROM LIFE

LIFE ON THE PLAYGROUND

Until recently, I dreaded going to the playground with my daughter, Sophia. Ever since she learned to walk, I felt compelled to watch her every move like a hawk, desperate to make sure she wouldn't fall off the jungle gym and crack her skull open or break her little arms and legs. I wasn't the world's greatest athlete as a child, and when Sophia learned how to go down steps, I cringed every time she put one foot in front of the other. I couldn't banish the image from my mind of her tumbling down the short staircase next to the baby slide. My only moments of peace were spent at the baby swings because I could be in complete control of my daughter's experience. To make matters worse, with a few exceptions, I found the other mothers and babysitters to be unfriendly, distracted, and extremely tense. Some days were better than others, but in general, I would have preferred to go to the dentist or the gynecologist than to the playground. Many mothers of children Sophia's age, including my pediatrician, confirmed my feeling that the playground was an unfriendly and dangerous place. I concluded—against all my spiritual training and my intuition—that my perception was *real*, which left me hopelessly doomed to pretend to have fun, season after season, while secretly agonizing over my daughter's well being.

One morning, for some reason, I woke up in a good mood and decided that we should go to the playground. The weather was nice; Sophia had already been there many times with her babysitters and had not come home with even one small injury, so I decided to give the playground another chance. When we got there, it was soon obvious that Sophia didn't need me to hover behind her anymore. She was going to be three in July and was an old pro now. She showed off by swinging from the bars on the jungle gym and running really fast. My daughter was the big boss and dictated my role to me. She didn't want me sitting on the sidelines observing. Oh no, I was going to be an active participant. I must have counted to ten a million times as Sophia and three other kids played a never-ending and totally enjoyable game of hide and seek with me as the designated "seeker." We drew pictures with sidewalk chalk, slid down the slide, and finally sat down for lunch—all without a scraped knee or even a single scary image popping into my head. As we headed home, I realized that the same people from last year were at the playground, but they seemed happier, friendlier, and more relaxed. I was thrilled with

Sophia's budding independence and totally delighted that the playground had changed so much in one short year. The best part of it all was that I didn't have to do one damn thing to make it happen. On the playground, things just naturally take care of themselves.

Tami

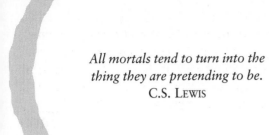

All mortals tend to turn into the thing they are pretending to be.
C.S. LEWIS

Question 26

Are you a body, mind, or soul?

We hear a lot about balancing ourselves physically, mentally, and spiritually. That's because most of us tend to favor one of these aspects over the other two. We've created the following quiz to help you discover whether your main approach to life stems from your body, mind, or soul. Answer the following questions to determine your spiritual profile.

1. **What do you most enjoy reading?**
   a. romantic novels
   b. the latest article about an unexplained scientific phenomenon
   c. a nonfiction account of someone's life experience

2. **Would you be most insulted if someone thought you were:**
   a. intellectually inferior
   b. not so good looking
   c. neither, you don't really care what other people think

3. **Which activity do you enjoy most?**
   a. discussing politics/religion/the latest episode of *Sex and the City*
   b. creating a new recipe/painting/way of doing something
   c. ordering a new toy/dress/piece of furniture from your favorite store

4. **You see two people arguing very aggressively on the street, your first instinct is to:**
   a. ignore it—it's none of your business
   b. stay out of the way—in case the situation gets out of hand
   c. stop to listen and find out what they are fighting about

5. **When you read a story like *Alice in Wonderland*, you are most likely to:**
   a. try and figure out the social and political satire behind the story
   b. be entranced by this bizarre land with surreal characters
   c. draw some meaning or moral from Alice's experiences

6. Which best describes your attitude in the face of opposition?
   a. I always fight to protect what's mine
   b. I try to compromise first, but I would fight for justice if I had to
   c. I first look for the lesson to be learned from the situation, the solution usually becomes clear after that

7. What do you want your epitaph on your tombstone to read?
   a. (s)he lived life the way (s)he wanted to
   b. (s)he was good looking up till the end
   c. (s)he accomplished everything (s)he needed to do

SCORING

Question	a	b	c
1. What do you most enjoy reading?	body	mind	soul
2. Would you be most insulted if someone thought you were:	mind	body	soul
3. Which activity do you enjoy more?	mind	soul	body
4. You see two people arguing very aggressively on the street, your first instinct is to:	soul	body	mind
5. When you read a story like *Alice in Wonderland* you are most likely to:	mind	body	soul
6. Which one best describes your attitude in the face of opposition?	body	mind	soul
7. What do you want your epitaph on your tombstone to read?	soul	body	mind

Count the total number of body, mind, and soul answers. Whichever has the greatest number is your dominant profile.

RESULTS

Body
You are a body type, living your life largely in relation to your physical self. A focus on the body can manifest itself in a variety of ways from an intense need to protect and preserve your body to strong delight in physical pleasures like sports, eating, or sex. Body types feel right at home in the material world. You also tend to believe that without your body, you are nothing. Be aware that if you focus too much energy on your physical self, you may overlook your true spiritual nature.

Mind
You are a mind type, living your life largely in relation to your thoughts and intellect. A focus on the intellect often manifests in an analytical approach to the world around you. While your ability to reason helps you to accomplish a great deal, beware of getting too bogged down in interesting theories to notice that above all, you are a spiritual being.

Soul
You are a soul type, living your life largely in relation to your spiritual self. A focus on the soul manifests itself in a tendency to see all things as connected. You tend to believe that everything happens for a reason and that the reason is worth exploring. You value experience and knowledge above all else, and have spent time testing your spiritual beliefs to know if they make sense. Your challenge is to learn to deal effectively with others who are more focused on their bodies and minds.

Men are tormented by the opinions they have of things, not by the things themselves.
MICHEL DE MONTAIGNE

Question 27

How is it possible to be spiritual when we live in such a tough world?

AIDS, poverty, fascist regimes, depression, racism, war. Why would anyone want to sugarcoat these ugly realities by praising the "divine" power that caused them—*if* such a power even exists? Ironically, the very act of writing the world off because we don't like what we see is what makes the situation so utterly hopeless. You know the old saying, "If you don't vote, you have no right to complain about who's in office?" The electoral system (despite its flaws) was not designed to support a particular party or agenda—it's a procedure for directing our individual power toward achieving what we want in society. Similarly, life is impartial, and only takes on meaning when we decide how to direct it. If we don't make an effort to nourish the good in life through our thoughts, words, and actions, then we shouldn't be surprised when the world appears to be a very tough place. It takes courage and initiative to look for the good. Sometimes the positive aspect of a situation is latent— only to be realized when someone (maybe you) takes constructive action to help. But, if all we do is sit around talking about how bad things are, we do nothing to lift ourselves or anyone else out of the rotten situation. The weight of the world lessens only when we acknowledge our own power to effect even the smallest change, and focus our energy on doing so. When enough people do the same, we see solutions to problems on a global level. That's the point of being spiritual.

A PAGE FROM LIFE

I AND THE VILLAGE

The Jewish Museum in New York City had an exhibit of the early works of the artist Marc Chagall. The paintings, many of which had never been shown before in North America, were from the period when Chagall lived in his hometown of Vitebsk, which was then part of the Russian Empire. My grandfather on my mother's side came from this same town and was roughly of the same generation. Living as a Jew in Russia in the late 1800s was no picnic. Chagall found solace in art, and my grandfather's family found salvage in bootleg alcohol, which they produced for the Cossacks in exchange for not having their house burned down. But eventually, the political situation became too severe to control with vodka, and the family decided to flee.

Pop always told us stories about his trip from Russia as a young boy of maybe ten years old. He came on a large ship and his most vivid memory of the passage was the awful smell. The boat stopped in London where Pop saw a department store for the first time. The sight of Harrods was so spectacular that he never forgot it. The family arrived in New York at Ellis Island—the classic immigration story. My grandfather had conjunctivitis and was detained at immigration until a relative already in New York came to claim him, bringing with her proof that she had the means to take care of him. Pop used to talk about Chagall as if they were old buddies even though they had never met. When we were young kids, he would tell us that Chagall's famous painting *I and the Village* was of his hometown in Russia. I pictured my grandfather running around fields of blue with cows flying in the air and crooked roofs on all the little houses like in the painting.

As Pop got older, the stories of his ties to Chagall became more involved. Sometime in the 1970s, he tried writing to Chagall in Paris. Pop said he wanted to thank him for inspiring his family to leave the *shtetl*. But the address was incorrect and the letter was returned. Then in the 1980s, the Philadelphia Museum of Art had a huge Chagall exhibit that coincided with the artist's death. My mother and I took Pop and drove down to Philly. We asked him all sorts of questions about the "old country." "Is this what it looked like?" "Did your family have cows?" "Did the Cossacks ever come to your house?" Our curiosity was endless. Pop looked at a few of the paintings and summed it all up for us. "You know," he said, "I was a little boy when we left, and I really don't remember that much." So much for family history. For his birthday, sometime in his late 80s, I gave him a calendar with Chagall's paintings and he looked me right in the eyes and said, dramatically, "Of all the artists in the world, you picked Chagall. He was responsible for me coming to the United States." And then he bowed his head and took pause. By the time my grandfather was in his 90s, it was almost as if Chagall had lead him by the hand to Ellis Island.

Although Pop tried to ascribe a certain amount of fantasy to the story, I knew that his family lived through a time of danger and uncertainty, and for this, I have always felt sadness. There are a lot of seemingly awful events that can destroy the body and wound the spirit, but, to me, actions motivated by hatred are the hardest to understand. Unfortunately, my grandfather's story isn't unique. I met a holocaust survivor for the first time in high school. He was the father of a friend—a nice man whose demeanor would never have revealed his past. I was stunned and sad—incredibly sad for what he had endured. And so it has been with people all around the world. *Angela's Ashes*, a stunning story of survival and hope, left me with a knot in my stomach and filled with empathy for the Irish poor. Similarly, stories of my father-in-law's family trying to leave Shanghai before the onset of the communist revolution leave me speechless. But in fact, the people I met and heard about were the lucky ones. They survived and went on to lead relatively good lives, while many more never made it or still live in horrible conditions today.

This sadness of the world touched me very deeply as a kid, and I really wanted to understand how people could treat each other so cruelly. My grandfather's musings often annoyed me because I wanted more facts—I wanted more information about what had happened to him and how he got through it. Somehow, if I could just analyze the situation, maybe I could figure it out and control it, at least in my own mind. But he never really wanted to talk about anything too serious. I think I was more interested in his past than he was.

As an adult, I came to the conclusion that I had to let some of this sadness go, or it would paralyze me. So I turned my attention to less emotional, more impartial topics. I became a scientist, and although it lacked a certain human warmth, the consistency of physical laws was a great comfort to me. I studied what happened to buildings during earthquakes, and was able to watch footage of spectacular devastation with a clear objectivity. The water table was high, the quake shook the earth, the water caused the soil to liquefy and the building collapsed to the ground. It was powerful and destructive, but it was also lawful and impersonal. Somehow it was a lot easier for me to ask, "OK, what can we do about this problem?" when I didn't take the problem personally. I didn't say, "How dare the earth tremble and hurt all of those innocent people!" It was tragic at times, but I knew that the earth was impartial and erupted wherever and whenever physical stresses needed to be released.

I like to think that some of my work contributed to building safer structures somewhere in the world. This feeling of accomplishment is in sharp contrast to the hopelessness I feel under the spell of human persecution.

Maybe Pop's lighthearted attitude about the old days was his way of not taking it personally. I realize now that it was wrong of me to expect him to own up to an experience that, in truth, was not worth owning. He never denied his heritage or who he was, but he refused to identity with an awful past, and maybe this refusal is what kept his past from becoming his future.

Karen

Question 28

What does it mean to be spiritual when everyone around me is acting like an idiot?

Once you decide to live a more peaceful life, the first thing you notice is that most people around you are not on the same wavelength. You realize that just because *you've* made changes, doesn't mean that your family and friends are dying to do the same. In fact, they're probably a bit pissed off that you're not the same miserable person they used to commiserate with. Does this mean that you can't associate with them anymore? No, but it'll take some fortitude to weather the transition period that follows any major self-change.

The first step is to have compassion. We are all limited by our beliefs and life experiences. If those around you have never turned a situation around by changing their own inner attitude, then they may not understand where your newfound "positivity" comes from. The second step is to look at yourself honestly. Their behavior is irksome because you are still susceptible to bouts of negativity. If you're serious about living more peacefully, then you have to deal with others more peacefully and accept that they have different ways of doing things. But, and here's the key, while you adapt on one level, on another you let go. When someone acts like an idiot, the ability to laugh, sympathize, or accept him or her without judgment, keeps you from being dragged down. It may take some effort at first, but eventually, you'll get your spiritual "sea legs," and outside influences will no longer disturb your inner peace so easily. Once you set your own course along the path of peace, you'll attract new people and situations more in keeping with your new perspective. You'll also find it easier to maintain relationships with some of the long-time "negative Nellies" who are important in your life, and you'll appreciate them all the more for having put up with your "idiot" moments along the way.

And yet I wish but for the thing I have:
My bounty is as boundless as the sea,
My love as deep; the more I give to thee,
The more I have, for both are infinite.
JULIET
ROMEO & JULIET BY WILLIAM SHAKESPEARE

Question 29

Where's my soulmate?

Our culture is obsessed with the idea of romantic love, but the real life process of finding the "right" person can be frustrating. While some people have a difficult time finding lovers, others never seem to be without a steady stream of suitors. But either way, "true love" often remains elusive. On the deepest level, all people long for union with the beloved. And while merging with the divine is the one true goal, there is no doubt that curling up in front of a fire with a real person has its merits. Finding love does not have to be an impossible dream. Try the following method and see what happens.

1. **Create an Image**
    The physical dimension is a reflection of our inner world, therefore, if we want something, we have to create a detailed picture of what we want and believe that we can get it. Let's start with the image—write down all of the attributes you want in a lover. Include the following details:

    a. Physical traits, such as age, height, weight, and any details about health or physical abilities you'd like your partner to have.

    b. Profession/occupation, financial status, and any lifestyle issues that are important to you, such as whether you want to live in a house/apartment, in the city/country/suburbs, with/without kids, etc.

    c. Mental and emotional qualities, such as intelligence, education, introvert/extrovert, kind, loving, compassionate, accepting, etc.

    d. Religious/Spiritual beliefs.

2. **Become the Image**
    Next, transform yourself into your image. For example, if you want an athletic, financially secure, loving, city dweller, then do your best to fit this image into your own life—get off the couch, save a few bucks every week, be nice to yourself and others, and spend some time in town. Then, through the law of attraction—like attracts like—you'll set the energies in motion to manifest your image. If it's

not that easy to do, don't despair. Most of us have complex and sometimes contradictory beliefs about love that are often deeply buried in our unconscious minds. Sometimes these beliefs are about our own self worth, "I'm afraid to be loving until I'm sure my love will be returned" and sometimes they're just common contradictions, "I want someone who is very successful, but I hate it when they spend all their time at work." The best way to find out what you *really* believe about love is to try and become your version of the perfect lover. If you can't become what you want to attract, you have two choices: get real—adjust your image to more closely match who you are now, or get moving—change your beliefs about who you are. Either way, you come out ahead.

A PAGE FROM LIFE

THE LOVE OF MY LIFE

Giuseppe Scorcia is the love of my life. We found each other in a bar on Houston Street in New York City a few months after I turned thirty-one. I had always been a bit afraid of bars, so it never crossed my mind that I might meet my soulmate in one. My snobbery (and lack of understanding of the laws of nature) led me to believe that I would meet my Prince in a more upscale venue, perhaps the Museum of Modern Art or Versailles. Anyway, it was Bastille Day, and I was with my dear Franco-American buddy, Lucinda. We were speaking en français and I was surprised and happy that my end of the conversation flowed, thanks, no doubt, to a few glasses of chardonnay. Giuseppe, who was also one of Lucinda's buddies, came over to me and also began to speak French. I was thrilled that he thought I was French and even more excited when I discovered that he was Italian. I never realized how deep my attraction was for foreign men until my mother reminded me that I informed her, while just a child, that I wasn't going to marry an American. I still wonder what made me reject my countrymen at such a young age, perhaps part of me already knew how my story would unfold.

Even as I spoke to Giuseppe for the first time, I knew that he was someone special. I had an immediate problem, however. I was on the rebound from a relationship with a man I had really loved. He wasn't foreign, but he did have one magical quality that I feared I'd never find again. In addition to speaking French and Spanish, he spoke Brazilian Portuguese. Most women like a man with money or oceanfront property, but I like a guy who can talk with the natives of what I think is the world's most diverse and beautiful country. My head might be French, but my heart is Brazilian. As a child, I had visited Brazil and had fallen in love with the people, the landscape, and the culture. I loved the language so much that I studied it for three years in college and when my boyfriend and I broke up, I sobbed hysterically to my friend Julia, "I'll never meet another man who speaks Portuguese." Julia told me that I would and I believed her.

After a few weeks of chatting on the phone, I decided it was time to make a move on Giuseppe. Since I am a graduate of a woman's college, I asked him out. We talked for hours and as we were crossing Seventh Avenue at Bleecker Street, he mentioned that he had lived and worked in Brazil. I thought I hadn't heard him correctly. I said, "Do you speak Portuguese?" "Of course," he replied. My heart stopped.

After the Portuguese disclosure, I let myself fall in love with this most wonderful and generous man. But the incident that sealed the deal still shakes me up when I think about it. As we were driving on the Long Island Expressway, we were talking about Pittsburgh, my home-town. Giuseppe said, "Once, on my way to West Virginia, I stopped in Pittsburgh to check out a place called The Institute for the Study of Cycles. Have you ever heard of it?" I screamed so loud I thought he was going to crash the car. When I calmed down, I explained that as a teenager, I had been so deeply affected by a not so popular book called *Cycles: The Mysterious Forces that Trigger Events* by Edward R. Dewey and Og Mandino that I became a member of the Institute he was talking about. I had never visited the Institute, but I was so engrossed in the subject that my family still teases me about it to this day. Giuseppe, who we later figured out probably made the trip to the Institute about the same time I was reading the book, was also strongly affected by the subject. As soon as I got home from our expedition to Long Island, I called my parents to tell them the story. They were stunned. "Who else, but your man," they said, "would speak Brazilian Portuguese and have read that book?"

Giuseppe and I have many other things in common. He has an MBA in marketing, and soon after I met him I became the marketing coordinator for a law firm. We're both passionate about music and theater. We share similar political and religious views. We both study Concept-Therapy. Right before we made our first trip to his hometown in Italy, I had a vivid (and accurate) dream about one of the neighboring towns even though I had never been there. When all is said and done, however, it's our differences that provide the final proof of our compatibility. Giuseppe is very comfortable in the physical dimension, quite fearless in fact. He is also unbelievably patient. I'm an intuitive but impatient person. In the ten years we've been together, he has helped me feel more comfortable in the "real" world, and thanks to his example, my patience has improved considerably—which is a profound gift.

I can now see that it took me thirty-one years to find Giuseppe because my image of myself, and therefore of him, wasn't complete enough until that time. Every day, when I look into my beautiful husband's eyes, the truth of the One Life Principle is revealed to me. We are not two halves that make up one whole. We are one.

Tami

*When some misfortune threatens,
consider seriously and deliberately what
is the very worst that could possibly happen.
Having looked this possible misfortune in
the face, give yourself sound reasons for
thinking that after all it would be no such
terrible disaster. Such reasons always exist, since
at the worst nothing that happens to
oneself has any cosmic importance.*
BERTRAND RUSSELL
THE CONQUEST OF HAPPINESS

question 30

Want to learn the art of triangular thinking?

Most of us, whether we realize it or not, have a negative view of life. It's not really our fault; we've been trained that way since infancy. We're raised to be cautious, good children who never talk to strangers for fear that our pictures will be immortalized on the backs of milk cartons everywhere. When we get older, our religions reinforce the idea that bad things happen to good people (take one more look at Jesus on the cross). Our education does a great job at keeping the fear going (remember the "permanent record file" that was going to follow you to your grave?) By the time we get into the work world, we're scared stiff, but well prepared for never-ending, steady doses of financial, emotional, and medical stress. Sound familiar?

Believe it or not, there is actually a simple way out of this one-sided perspective on reality. Learn to master the art of triangular thinking. Instead of giving your mind carte blanche to forever travel the negative highway, retrain your brain to see things in a more open-ended way. In any situation, it is our choice to see things as positive, negative, or neutral. This is the triangular perspective on material reality. Because we believe that we are first and foremost material beings, we tend to categorize everything in life as good, bad, or indifferent in relation to how it affects us, not by what it really is in essence. For example, most people would categorize a severe flood as a "bad" thing, and for the people directly affected, it sure seems pretty horrible. But for the thousands of relief workers around the world, who tirelessly work to help others in times of disaster, this is an opportunity to do "good." Those of us not involved remain pretty much oblivious, especially if we haven't read the paper or watched the news for days. On an even more profound level, the flood is simply a natural and periodic occurrence. In other words, it just "is." The key to the triangular approach is to play with it until we clearly see that events take on the significance we assign to them. When faced with a crisis such as a flood, rather than panic, we can choose to adopt the purposefulness of a relief worker or find some spiritual objectivity to get us through the crisis. Give yourself a rest from the doom and gloom. Life is not a straight line, with good and bad or life and death at each end. It is more like a triangle. So, get out there and explore a new corner.

Arlene Weissman, 2000

Part 3

A Kick-Ass View of Reality

In Parts 1 and 2, we saw how changing our perspective alters our reality. This is our spiritual power, and it's the key to getting what we want, and getting out of what we don't want. But it's a kick in the ass. Opinions once held so strongly, become questionable and, ultimately, dispensable. Part 3 is an invitation to continue breaking down limiting ideas, but at the same time, to start having fun with our newfound ability to see different sides of an issue. When we're not shackled to our beliefs, life becomes a lot more interesting.

THE GEMINI 4 SPACE WALK
On June 3, 1965, Gemini 4 astronaut
Ed White became the first American to step
outside his spacecraft and let go. After the first
three minutes the fuel ran out in the gas pow-
ered hand gun used to propel him, and White
maneuvered by twisting his body and pulling
on the 8 meter long umbilical cord that fed
him oxygen from the spacecraft.
NATIONAL SPACE SCIENCE DATA CENTER
NASA GODDARD SPACE FLIGHT CENTER

Question 31

Who's at the other end of your umbilical cord?

We all have a source of power that nourishes us throughout our lives, like a fetus is fed through an umbilical cord. If we are aware of this, we can choose to connect our cord to something great like the wisdom of the ages or the power of Nature, which can create anything from ideas to mountains (some people call this power God). The tricky part, however, is that as we leave the womb and become more involved with our individuality, we lose sight of the big universe from whence we came and start to connect our cord to other sources of power that may not serve us as well. Many of us connect to temporal things—our jobs, homes, families, health, looks, abilities—things that fade in time or that sometimes are abruptly taken away from us. An unfortunate few connect to nothing at all and fall into despair or a lifelong use of anti-depressants. What are you connected to that sustains you in life? Who or what is at the other end of your umbilical cord? It's worth considering every now and then, if only to remind yourself that you are part of a big powerful universe, and that some of that power just may be flowing into your navel right now.

*Put your hand on a hot stove for a minute,
and it seems like an hour. Sit with a pretty
girl for an hour, and it seems like a minute.
That's relativity.*
ALBERT EINSTEIN

Question 32

If time is such a relative concept, why do we let it dictate our lives so absolutely?

Time is not a real thing. It's a clever tool we invented for making plans with other people, as in "let's meet for drinks at eight." But often we take it too far and let time define our development. Every new idea, every goal, needs a period of gestation, and the truth is not everyone is on the same timetable. Did you ever get so involved in something that you didn't even realize how much time had passed? It's situations like this when we are truly in touch with our own instinct about the value of what we are doing. When we start comparing ourselves to others or to some "statistically based" time frame, then we begin to doubt ourselves and cut ourselves off from our own intuition. So next time you proclaim your faith that your luck will change with your new positive outlook, don't get angry when it doesn't change overnight. Show the spiritual life force that you mean business by sticking with your resolution until life responds.

A PAGE FROM LIFE

CHRISTMAS ISLAND TIME

On our honeymoon in 1994, my husband and I went to a remote island in the Pacific called Christmas Island. It's part of the Republic of Kiribati (pronounced *Kiribas*), which, until 1999, was split down the middle by the International Date Line. This was the first major clue that "time" was altogether a different concept here. Air Nauru makes a weekly round trip from Honolulu to the nation of Nauru, stopping at Christmas Island along the way. You come in on a Tuesday and can leave the following Monday—if you're lucky. As we waited to board our flight at the Honolulu airport, the agent explained that on the island everything happens more slowly. Our flight was interesting, a bit disconcerting, and quite humorous. The pilot and copilot took turns resting in the main cabin where they were served lunch by the flight attendants. When we landed, we were asked to remain on the plane for "insect control," which consisted of a barefoot man in shorts spraying the overhead bins with a small can of *Raid*.

After a week of fly fishing for bonefish, more my husband's sport than mine, I was ready to get off the island. We had just finished a farewell lunch with our host at his guesthouse in London—the island only has three towns, London, Paris, and Banana—when the telegraph officer came over to tell us that our plane has been delayed. "How long?" we asked, thinking it was a good thing we had a twelve-hour layover in Honolulu before our next flight. "I don't know," he said. We tried rephrasing the question. "What's the longest the plane has ever been delayed?" "Five weeks," he responded.

As information about the source of the delay trickled in over the next couple of days, we learned that the King of Nauru needed the plane to take his soccer team to a tournament, so we would be stuck there with our food supply dwindling until they lost a match, or, worse yet, made it to the tournament finals at the end of the week. It turned out to be a four day delay—not bad compared to five weeks, but still long enough to cause us to miss our connecting flight and lose all our subsequent reservations. When we returned to Honolulu, the same agent who prophetically warned us about the slower pace of the islands greeted us and then spent the next few days rebooking the rest of our eight-week trip. Grumbling about the mishap, we didn't see much value in this disregard for time.

Six years later, the international dateline was moved over to bring Christmas Island into the same time zone as the rest of Kiribati. This group of islands was the first nation to greet the year 2000 and its sunrise ceremonies were broadcast around the world. The soothing music and peaceful speeches of the Kiribati people stood out amid the nervousness and threats of terrorism that plagued much of the industrialized world as the midnight hour approached. It was then I realized that such eloquent simplicity is hard to come by in a nation where the planes always land on time.

Karen

Question 33

Can a little narcissism be good for the soul?

Authentic self-love is the highest expression of the One Life Principle. But we live in a world where duality is king. As a result of the powerful illusion that we are separate and different from each other and our Creator, it can be difficult to feel love at all, much less the unconditional, pure love that comes from union with all that is. The spiritual quest, the journey to the One, is a roller coaster ride through the seemingly impenetrable walls we've built to preserve and enhance our shaky sense of self and our insecure attachment to our uniqueness and individuality. We humans are complicated characters. Our animal nature wants nothing more than survival; quality of life issues do not enter into the picture. Our psyche wants protection (and sometimes revenge) from the nasty bastards who would deprive us of a "healthy ego." But our spiritual nature wants nothing from external reality because it knows there's no such thing. It simply propels us forward, despite (or maybe because of) the obstacles our animal and psychic natures put in our way. It urges us to love, to accept, to heal, to let go once and for all, so that eventually we'll be able to see what we've been the whole time—perfect little indestructible sparks of God.

"Your mother and brothers are outside, asking for you." And he [Jesus] replied, "Who are my mother and brothers?" And looking around on those who sat about him, he said, "Here are my mother and my brothers! Whosoever does the will of God is my brother, and sister, and mother."
MARK 3: 32-35

question 34

Are you my mother?

Remember the children's book *Are You My Mother?* by P.D. Eastman? It's a great story about a little bird, who, when he hatches discovers that his mother isn't there to take care of him. He goes out to look for her, but because he doesn't know what she looks like, he walks right past her. He asks various animals if any of them were his mother to no avail. In the end, the baby bird returns to the nest. Now that he's gained some life experience, he knows he's a bird and recognizes his mother when she arrives with a worm for him to eat. This story is simple, but the message is spiritually profound: until we know who *we* are, we can't recognize anyone else for who they really are. It is no secret that life is a journey with many ups and downs. Sometimes we get so caught up in the supposed wrong turns we think we've taken that we end up blaming our parents for our "mistakes." While this is understandable given our modern propensity for assigning blame, it is a distraction that slows us down and keeps us from seeing the big picture. We alone are responsible for our lives, whether our mothers were there for us or not. This idea may not be comforting, but it's intensely liberating. If we are completely responsible for ourselves, then we are free to choose the life we want to live and are not obligated to fulfill any role or make anyone else happy. Once we see life as an adventure of self-exploration rather than as a series of traumas inflicted on us by others, we are free to transcend our childhoods and see our parents as they really are, spiritual beings just like ourselves who are struggling to understand how things work.

question 35

Is there sex after death?

We are a severely conflicted species. We talk about the importance of a healthy sex life, yet, as children, most of us were discouraged from masturbating, brainwashed to fear physical intimacy and encouraged to "just say no." Repressing the natural sexual instinct does not result in a higher degree of morality as our Judeo-Christian ethics would have us believe. Instead, it creates the conditions for a distorted and pornographic view of sexuality that equates the act of physical loving with violence and death. We even think we've evolved because talking about death isn't taboo anymore. But how advanced are we, really? In war, we mourn our own dead while we use the latest technology to kill our enemies. We prosecute people who believe in a terminally ill patient's right to die while we prepare for the next criminal execution. We spend millions of dollars "educating" the public about the need for ongoing disease detection in the form of yearly mammograms, pap smears, and prostate exams in order to prevent death, but we can't seem to figure out why so much cancer occurs in the sex organs. As shocking as it sounds, could "just say no" be at the root of the problem?

We are both biological and spiritual creatures. The sexual urge is also the creative urge and is the means by which life creates and sustains itself. When we allow ourselves to love—emotionally, physically, and spiritually—we surrender to life and experience the oneness of existence. It's ironic, but when we die, we also surrender. Maybe that's why the French call the orgasm "the little death." It is through surrender that we experience the One Life and learn that, despite appearances, there is no death. It is neither healthy nor spiritual to be rigid, ascetic, and afraid. The next time you feel the urge to live, love, or let go, just say yes.

A PAGE FROM LIFE

MY WORLD TRADE CENTER

I sit here almost two weeks after the terrorist attack on the World Trade Center thinking about my life. Like everyone else, my emotions have run the gamut from anger to depression—and it's not over yet as our government prepares for the war on terrorism. It will take at least six months to dig out the rubble from the collapse of the World Trade Center—the anchor of the New York City skyline. Each time I look down Seventh Avenue, I want to cry. Of course, I grieve for the people who died in the attack and for those who lost friends and family, but I can't believe I'm mourning a piece of real estate. Why am I so attached to this man-made symbol of power and might? After all, I always thought the Twin Towers were down right ugly on an aesthetic level. What is going on?

The World Trade Center might not have been beautiful, but whenever I saw the towers from a distance, I felt comforted, protected, and safe. Each time I drove back from Pittsburgh, my hometown, which is just eighty miles from the crash site of the fourth hijacked plane, my heart would leap as soon as the Twin Towers came into view. New York is my adopted home, the city of my adulthood. I've lived here longer than anywhere else and I now proudly consider myself to be a New Yorker. I'm not a patriotic person, but I'm intensely in love with the Big Apple, its energy and inhabitants. I've come into my own here. I've made my own way here. I met my husband here. I delivered my baby at St. Vincent's, the same hospital that desperately wanted to save lives in the wake of the disaster. I met Karen and became a Spiritual Chick here. New York has embraced me, encouraged me, and as I'm beginning to see more and more, reflected me. But New York isn't gone, only a part of downtown is crippled. Even the Stock Exchange is back up and running. I know they'll rebuild. Why do I feel so shaken up?

My first job in New York was a few doors down from the Stock Exchange, just off Wall Street. I worked as a paralegal in Richard Nixon's old law firm, which is kind of weird for a kid raised on antiwar rallies and the Watergate hearings. I told everyone that I was thinking of becoming a lawyer, but just two days into the job I knew there was no way. It's not that law isn't an admirable profession; it's just that I knew I'd be miserable. Down deep I knew that eventually my creative and artistic leanings would get the better of me. The atmosphere in a Wall Street law firm is intense; corporate lawyers are not the most relaxed people in the world. But then, neither am I, which is probably why I flourished there. I'm also adaptable. I've had to be. Within a year, I was promoted to supervisor. I was very proud that I was the youngest and had the least seniority of everyone on staff, yet I was their boss. My ego was flying high—maybe as high as the Towers.

A couple of years and a few promotions later, I left the law firm to begin a new career in midtown, far away from the soaring monoliths of the financial district. I became a headhunter in the accounting and finance field. I hated the job but made the decision not to give in to failure. Having permanently set foot on the spiritual path, I rallied all my strength and learned how to make one hundred cold calls a day and how to make money. After a year, I was fortunate enough to leave for a much better job on 59th Street as the Regional Director for a prestigious paralegal school located in Philadelphia. I worked closely with the home office, but for the most part, I called my own shots. I traveled, wrote articles for trade magazines and newsletters, and gave seminars. I developed my own style of career counseling and built a strong presence for the school in the New York area. I started taking more risks in my personal life and began taking voice lessons. Then, just as I hit my stride, personally and professionally, the company began to flounder and I decided to quit. I spent a miserable few months in another job in the placement field, but then made a leap of faith and stopped working to sing and to write a book with a dear friend. It nearly broke me. I cried every day. I didn't have any money coming in and I had a hard time handling my intense feelings of insecurity. And then the book fell through. My singing, my mother, and my friends sustained me. My spiritual quest intensified. When all seemed lost, the Twin Towers beckoned to me again.

I returned to the law firm where I first started my career. But the job wasn't on the same level as the one I left six years before. It was a giant blow to my ego. Where was the towering protection of the nearby World Trade Center? I would have to reearn that sense of security and well-being. Before I left the first time, the firm had relocated to a tall building that overlooked the East River. As a nonlawyer, however, I had an inner office with no view of the outside world. Even from my insulated location, I felt the rumbling of the 1993 bombing of the World Trade Center, but I stayed at work that day even after many had decided to leave the area, because my gut told me I was safe. I was paying attention to my intuition by this time and trying to bring my spiritual ideals in line with my day-to-day life, a goal I'm still trying to achieve. After this horrible event, something shifted inside me. I began to understand that change is inevitable and that I didn't have to take life so personally. My emotions weren't the reliable lens on the world that I thought they were. My view of the world was not based on objective fact; it was simply the result of my nature and my experience. I realized that if I wanted to be happy, I would have to let go of everything, and see what the world looked like then. As I began to let go, new opportunities appeared. Within a year, I had a new job in the firm as the communications coordinator and an office with a window. My view wasn't of the World Trade Center; my office faced east toward Brooklyn, the direction of the rising sun.

I left this job after a year. I had come to the end of the line. It was time for me to sing, to write, to live outside the protection of the past and out of the shadow of the World Trade Center. It was a gigantic symbol for me of external authority and a way of life that didn't work for me anymore. Ironically, not long after I left, the law firm where I came of age and that had just celebrated its 126th anniversary collapsed under the weight of too many egos. Six years later, the Trade Center is gone too, a victim of a bloody global war of egos. I wonder what they'll build in its place—what I'll build in its place.

Tami

If a woman has to choose between catching a fly ball and saving an infant's life, she will choose to save the infant's life without even considering if there is a man on base.
DAVE BARRY

Question 36

Why can't a woman be more like a man?

There's a blunt Yiddish expression that loosely translates as "If the grandmother had balls, she'd be the grandfather." It's used to imply that "if" is not a very reliable condition, but we think it also answers our question. Every creative process requires two key elements—the idea and the execution, the seed and the germination, the customer who wants a new bathroom and the contractor who builds it. As humans, we've labeled ourselves and all other organisms according to the part we play in the procreation of the species—the male has the big idea and the female carries it out. In day-to-day life, however, each of us tends one way or the other, regardless of our gender. But any "idea man" who doesn't have the patience to wait for the execution gets nothing done, and any person who busies him or herself with activities without stopping to consider the objective won't have much to show for their efforts either. When the masculine and feminine principles are not in cooperation, within ourselves, among groups, or even between nations, we end up with a metaphoric battle of the sexes. It's like trying to grow a plant without a seed or build a bathroom without a builder. It won't work. The process of thinking followed by action is a working model for our creative universe. Master this art and nothing is impossible, but deny it and we cut ourselves off from the potential to harmonize with all creative power. So any time we wish that the yin in the world were more like our yang, or vice-versa, remember, if all the grandmothers had balls, there'd be no grandkids!

Question 37

Want to live in hell?
If you lived there you'd
be home now.

The good news is that hell isn't some subterranean
torture chamber run by demons with pitchforks. The bad
news is that it's a whole lot closer to home. In his play
No Exit, Jean-Paul Sartre said, "Hell is other people."
And he's right, in the sense that other people mirror our
own state of mind back to us every minute of every day
without interruption. When we entertain feelings of hate,
anger, jealousy, envy, greed, fear, criticism, vanity, deceit,
selfishness, worry, or prejudice, we are in hell, surrounded
by devils in the form of other people. But when we
entertain feelings of love, patience, duty, noninterference,
kindness, faith, sympathy, courage, forgiveness, aspiration,
generosity, and hope, we are in heaven surrounded by

angels. All the great spiritual traditions teach that our fundamental nature is spiritual, not material. Therefore, when we completely identify ourselves with material reality and deny (consciously or unconsciously) our true spiritual identity, we are in hell. Simply put, hell is a moment-by-moment choice—not a location. If you're in hell right now, don't despair, you can be in heaven in the blink of an eye.

A PAGE FROM LIFE

JOURNEY TO THE SOUL

I've been having some high-level discussions with the devil
It turned into one helluva debate
It wasn't easy, but I convinced him to take your case
While he refused to make predictions about the outcome of your fate
He said you were gonna have to learn to swim against the current
Or get used to being some bigger fish's bait

The other day I met with the big guy—you know the one I mean
He tried to change the course of history
It started with his mother, an angel and a dream
I brought your situation to his attention, thought he might dismiss you out of spite

He pondered for a little while before he turned
to me and said,
"I hate to admit it, but the Prince of Darkness
is absolutely right"

You know I've talked to many others, some of
them lesser known
Buddha, Krishna, Allah, even Jehovah didn't
know
They tried to find an escape route—a way out
of your living hell
The discussion went on for hours so I finally
broke the spell
Everyone could empathize with the nature of
your plight,
But not one of them could save you from this
necessary fight

It's quite a hard trip, this journey to the soul
Sometimes the reflection in the mirror seems
to mock you and all the lies you've told
I just got used to stumbling in the dark about
a half an hour ago
If I could lend a hand, I would—I've tried to
intervene
But when all is said and done my love, you've
got to find your own road
All the rest is just a dream

Tami

Technology is the knack of so arranging the world that we do not experience it.
MAX FRISCH

question 38

Who needs spiritual connection when I have the Internet?

From the light bulb to nuclear weapons, from the cotton gin to genetically modified foods, technology has always been a double-edged sword. The prevailing attitude is that technology makes us better, stronger, and more comfortable as long as it doesn't kill us, or morally bankrupt us, in the process. While scientific advancement seems to fall into the "can't live with it, can't live without it" category, the reason for this paradox may be more spiritual than we think. On the up side, technology exemplifies some of our highest ideals. If we are part of the One Life, which is all present, all powerful, and all knowing, then it's not that hard to figure out where we got the idea that we can breed our own plants, grow new body parts, and have access to any information, any time of day, in multiple languages. We are "playing God," so to speak, but as part of the One Life, isn't that our role to play? And yes, if things get out of hand, we may blow ourselves up in the process. But as strange as it may sound, that might not be the worst of it. After all, it's our bodies and minds that meet their demise; the infinite cosmic reality isn't going anywhere. The real danger comes when we scare ourselves into thinking that we are not complete without technology—that we are not eternal without plastic surgery or organ transplants, or that we cannot connect to each other without the Internet. Fear locks us into a sort of parallel universe in which technology mimics our "God-given" powers, but blinds us to the truth that the source of our creative power has been and always will be within us.

*Sooner murder an infant in its
cradle than nurse unacted desires.*
WILLIAM BLAKE,
THE MARRIAGE OF HEAVEN AND HELL

question 39

Is life a maximum security prison?

Well it sure as hell feels like it when you're not living the life you want to live. What stops us from expressing ourselves freely and openly on the job, in relationships, even when we're alone? What prevents us from actualizing our greatest dreams and aspirations? Fear, fear, and more fear. We're afraid others will disapprove of our secret longings. We're scared we're not good enough to be happy. We're petrified we won't be able to pay the mortgage, contribute to our 401(K), and do what we want to do at the same time. Under the powerful yoke of fear, life is literally a prison. But, like it or not, we play the roles of the jailor and the jailed at the same time. We may have inherited this fear of self-expression from our parents, teachers, religious leaders, politicians and bosses, but we're responsible for continuing the repression. We're free to walk out of the prison any time we choose. So put yourself on parole. Always wanted to sing? What's stopping you? You have a shower, don't you? Want to learn Swahili? Sign up for a class. Feel like trading in your running shoes for tap shoes? Do it. Don't analyze your need to express yourself or justify it to others. Life is not all about thinking things through. Does the sunflower think about whether or not to direct itself toward the sun? Does an infant weigh the pros and cons of whether to nurse at its mother's breast? Spirituality is not about holding back on our desires. It's about living our lives any damn way we want. Hallelujah.

A PAGE FROM LIFE

IF AT FIRST YOU DON'T SUCCEED

When I was in grade school, I had an experience that I will never forget. A girl in my class, who was large for her age and quite tough, began to talk back to the teacher in a somewhat belligerent manner. I don't remember what the argument was about, but my recollection is that the girl was not entirely to blame. Fearing that the situation was getting out of hand, the teacher asked the most obedient person in the class—me—to go and get the principal. I didn't want to be dragged into this mess, but the teacher was yelling at me to go, and I buckled and did as I was told. The principal came and hauled the girl off to his office, and as she was being dragged out of the classroom she looked at me and said "I'm gonna kick your ass for turning me in." I was petrified. I spent the next week at home "sick" until the situation blew over. But the worst part was that I knew the teacher had put me in a bad situation, but I had been afraid to buck authority.

Three years later, I was in my last year of Junior High School and it looked as though history was going to repeat itself. A girl in my class mouthed off to a neo-Nazi gym teacher who told her to change out of her uniform and head to the principal's office. Realizing that this girl was more likely to go have a cigarette in the locker room if left unattended, she turned to the most obedient person in the class—once again, me—to make sure that the condemned went to face her sentence. Oh, no, I thought, I wasn't going to fall into that trap again. My heart was pounding and my mouth was dry, but I managed to utter one word, "No." The teacher walked over to me and with all the compassion of a drill sergeant said, "What?" By now, everyone had dropped their volleyballs, and all eyes were on me. "It's not my responsibility to make sure that another kid gets punished," I said. She came even closer, looked down at me, and started screaming something about giving me one last chance to do what I'm told. I could feel her breath on my eyelashes, but I wasn't scared, and I didn't flinch. Finally, she told me I could escort my classmate to the principal's office, or I could go there myself. With the memory of my sixth grade incident indelibly fixed in my mind, her latter option was just fine with me. I left the gym floor and headed to the locker room where I promptly burst into tears. Through my heaving, I heard a voice. "Are you OK?" It was the bully, the one I was supposed to rat on. I looked at her and told her what happened, and she sat with me until I regained my composure. To my surprise, she was a nice kid, and to her surprise, I wasn't a total wimp.

Leaving the locker room, I headed for the payphone to call my mom. I had this idea that if she talked to the principal on my behalf things would go a little smoother. But she told me that I had handled it well up till that point, and she encouraged me to finish the job. While I was talking with her, the school bell rang and the halls filled with kids—kids who were knocking on the door of the phone booth giving me a thumbs-up for "telling off" the teacher. Apparently, I wasn't the only one who felt bullied by authority—even the kids who always talked back felt like no one was really listening to them.

I did go see the principal and, instead of pleading my case, I told him that the teacher owed me an apology. He said he wasn't sure if he could arrange that, but he told me not to worry about it and that he understood my point. I never got my apology, but I didn't get punished either. And the teacher, to her credit, didn't take it out on me during the rest of the school year. I learned not only that adults don't always know what's best, but also that I knew all along what was right for me. I was presented with two nearly identical situations where I knew what I should do, but one time I buckled under outside pressure, and one time I was true to myself. Both had repercussions, but the repercussions were much easier to take when I followed my own sense of what was right.

Karen

> *The coming of the Messiah does not depend upon anything supernatural, rather it depends upon human growth and self-transformation. The world will only be transformed when people realize that the Messiah is not someone other than themselves.*
> THE BAAL SHEM TOV

Question 40

Is there a messiah in the house?

It seems like we're constantly waiting to be rescued. Look at our culture. First, there's the notion of the prince in folk tales ranging from *Cinderella* to *Pretty Woman*. Next we have our love-hate relationship with the medical profession, which basically boils down to putting 100% of the responsibility for our health in the hands of a doctor who we will promptly turn around and sue if things don't turn out OK. And then we have our favorite, the lottery, that one-in-a-billion chance occurrence that will save us from our debts or our boring jobs and make our lives magical. This deeply rooted need to be saved is fundamental to many of the world's great religions. We're either waiting on someone to come take us out of this hell, or if he or she has already been here, we're waiting for them to return so we can get on with our lives as eternal beings. Meanwhile, we fall deeper and deeper into spiritual desolation until we have the equivalent of a spiritual heart attack and cry out "Help! Help! Is there a messiah in the house?" Now, no disrespect intended, but what if we assumed, for the time being, that there were no such saviors in our world or any other? If there were no doctors, we'd probably take better care of ourselves and start trusting our own instincts about our bodies. If there were no lottery, we'd probably have to find better jobs on our own, or at least come to terms with the one we have. And, if there were no Messiah, we'd have to look for enlightenment on our own. If all we're doing right now is sitting around waiting for deliverance, then it can't hurt to try and "save" ourselves. At the very least, we'll have something to talk about with the Messiah when he or she finally gets here.

Question 41

What's a little sin among friends?

Most people don't like being alone for long periods of time or being excluded from mainstream activities. Our deep need for the companionship of others is an unconscious, but driving force in our lives. No matter how strong we are in other ways, it's emotionally painful when there's no one there to comfort us in times of tragedy or to talk to when we're confused, afraid, or lonely. We're so aware of the spirit-breaking effects of prolonged isolation from other members of our species that we reserve solitary confinement for the most dangerous and resistant criminals. But it's not necessary to be a convict to feel the effects of isolation. Any time we don't fit in with the crowd because we're too short, too fat, not smart enough, or not the right class, race, gender, or ethnic background, we're deeply affected, and not for the better. It may sound overly simplistic, but behind every school shooting, terrorist attack, revolution, and holocaust are intense feelings of desperation and disenfranchisement—the result of a distorted desire to belong. Both the solitary, sociopathic actions of the Unabomber and the genocidal, mob mentality of the Nazi party are the ramifications of this desire taken to the extreme. Some say original sin is the cause of all of humanity's problems. They're right if we define original sin as the belief that we are separate from our divine source. There is only One Life. We're all made up of the same energy, come from the same place, and ultimately have the same destiny. We're all God's chosen people. Let's use our instinct to protect and preserve each other, not to separate and destroy.

A PAGE FROM LIFE

IT'S A MAD, MAD, MAD, MAD WORLD

I sit at the edge of a river in Nova Scotia with my laptop, while my husband, Alex, fly fishes. He searches for Atlantic salmon, but the occasional trout would also be fine. I don't like to fish much, but I enjoy writing on the sidelines. The view is spectacular, and a small tan fly accompanies me, loyally perched on the side of my screen. Perhaps he too enjoys the warmth of my computer on this cool, late summer day. Part of the reason that I don't like fishing is that it seems to hurt the fish for no good reason. Since I had salmon for dinner last night, eating the fish must qualify in some human-centric way as "good reason." But these days, North American fly fishing is mostly catch and release, and even where it's not required by law, Alex typically releases the fish, unharmed save for the tiny hole in its lip (from a barbless hook) which he says will heal in no time.

Alex and I have a running dialogue on the nature of the food chain and whether fishing constitutes cruel and unusual punishment versus a one of a kind alien-space-visitation-like experience for the fish. "What you may want to consider" he tells me, "is that each fish you hook is trying to eat another living creature when it goes after your fly, so don't feel so badly." An interesting thought. But to me this is a little like saying the death penalty is OK because you kill murderers—an argument I believe only propagates the idea of killing. But, he has a point. Evidence of carnivorous violence is everywhere in nature, and lions don't appear to lament the zebras they tear from limb to limb. So where do we draw the line between natural instinct and ethically evolved behavior? If there's one thing I am learning on this nature trip, it's that there are some pretty crazy things that go on in this world that are, in fact, totally natural.

Let's go back to the fish. When Atlantic salmon return to the river to spawn, they don't eat the entire time they are there—which can be as long as twelve months. This amazing feat of long distance swimming followed by procreation—all without any intake of food—is a marvel of nature. But the most likely function of this instinct is to protect the young salmon, either by preserving the food in the river for the growing parr, or by preventing the adult salmon from actually eating the parr. I was very impressed with this protective trigger until Alex told me about another breed of fish in which this trigger is not so foolproof. Large mouth bass refrain from eating for a shorter period than the salmon—up to two weeks—while they guard their hatching young. Once their appetite returns they eat whatever comes their way, which is sometimes their own offspring who have not yet grown large enough to protect themselves. I guess it goes to show that the workings of Nature are not personal. Birth and death, survival of the fittest, and the food chain apply even if it means a fish eats its own progeny.

Unlike animals, human beings are self-conscious individuals with the ability to reason and override our carnal instincts when our personal interests are at stake. Yet, every now and then we have a throwback to the animal kingdom that really offends our human sensibilities. On the radio yesterday we heard about a man who had just been granted unsupervised visitation rights with his baby and killed the child on the very first visit. This story is awful, but given the instincts of the fish, can we really say that it is "unnatural?" These baser instincts are part of our evolutionary heritage, so it's understandable that they will surface from time to time, causing us to forget that whatever we do to our fellow human beings we do to ourselves. But then again, the pain or the disappointment we feel in sympathy for those who were hurt reminds us of this connection again—so maybe there is a method to this madness.

There will always be events in life that defy human intelligence, but I am starting to accept that these occurrences are as natural as anything else we might experience. This acceptance gives me comfort. Not that I would ever stop trying to promote more humane action, but it's awfully painful (and terribly conceited) to think that the world is somehow defective because not everyone complies with my plea. It's as absurd as trying to talk a big fish out of eating a little fry.

Karen

> *Language can only deal meaningfully*
> *with a special, restricted segment of reality. The*
> *rest, and it is presumably the*
> *much larger part, is silence.*
> GEORGE STEINER

Question 42

What's in a name?

Imagine for a moment that we couldn't remember what anything was called, and that we had lost all pre-conceived notions of how things are supposed to be. We'd have to describe everything from the most fundamental frame of reference, making us aware of how we really think without the influence of conventional opinions. When we referred to people, we'd have to explain how they looked, how they talked, or how they made us feel. Going to the dentist might seem like a pleasant or at least a neutral experience because we'd have lost all sense that filling a cavity is *supposed* to be painful. The latest fashion might look totally bizarre, and the fact that it was purchased from the haute couture department at Barneys would not influence us in the least. We'd have to refrain from speaking about subjects that we don't understand well enough to describe, which would eliminate the need for cocktail parties worldwide. And while this "label amnesia" might make conversation cumbersome, it would free us to acknowledge that which has not yet been named, and to come face to face with all that is, just as it is.

Both theoretical scientists and the great mystics travel beyond language and current knowledge to explore new frontiers, and then struggle to describe that which is indescribable. The "quark," for example, is a label given to a theoretical concept that cannot, as of yet, be directly observed; the word heaven describes not a place but a potential state of being not yet experienced by the majority of people. New experiences often defy past definitions, so it is important to continually evaluate whether our knowledge, no matter how deeply entrenched it may be in conventional wisdom, is truly applicable to the new situation. This is how we move forward both scientifically and spiritually. It may seem like an arduous task to be so vigilant, but by thinking beyond the labels, we may be lucky enough to make a new discovery, and as a reward, we will get to name it.

It is always easier to fight for one's principles than to live up to them.
ALFRED ADLER

question 73

Are you a hypocrite?

We say we want peace and then we make war. We say we care about children, but we can't seem to end poverty. We tell ourselves to relax while we micromanage every second of our day, fearing what would happen if we had a minute without something to do. What is this conflict within the human soul that keeps us enslaved to our ideals but does not supply the energy to make them real? What is the cause of our self-deception and hypocrisy that brings us nothing but misery? At the core of our being, on a carnal level, is the desire for power and control over our environment. This is understandable. At the beginning of human history, survival was the name of the game. Those who could defeat the enemy and keep the community safe were the most important members of the group and commanded the most power.

From the earliest times, humans traded in their freedom for physical security and learned to fear what they didn't understand or couldn't control. But what was a necessity for primitive man brings nothing but pain to modern man. When we fear death, we can't help but crave the protection that external authority and conventional wisdom promise to provide. We'll work in jobs that we don't enjoy, even if we suffer from severe depression; we'll go to doctors who prescribe drugs to lift our mood and then discover that we never really heal. But, there is a solution. We need to find the courage to take back the power over our own lives and think for ourselves. All the false beliefs, shaky doctrines, scary scenarios, and allegiance to outside authority have to go. From a spiritual perspective, there is nothing external that needs to be overcome or controlled. If we want to overcome death, we must conquer our own carnal nature and choose everlasting life. When we're true to ourselves, we're in touch with the divine. We might be called heretics, but at least we won't be hypocrites.

A PAGE FROM LIFE

SINGING FOR MY LIFE

There are so many lifetimes
Hidden beneath the dust
I finally awakened
I heard the call
Now I won't stop
No longer up against the wall
One glorious moment I'll scream
I can't censor or rehearse
There isn't a person alive
Who can edit my dream
I'm singing for my life
Oh can't you see
Take it all from me now
Even that won't bother me
Cause I'm singing
I'm finally breathing
I'm singing for my life

Tami

That which is below is as that which is above, and that which is above is as that which is below, to accomplish the miracle of one thing.
HERMES TRISMEGISTUS
THE EMERALD TABLE

Question 44

Does electricity prove the existence of God?

At the core of hermetic philosophy is the axiom, "As above, so below; as below, so above." This philosophical precept speaks to the correspondence between the divine and the mundane, the macrocosm and the microcosm, the world of ideas and physical reality. It suggests that by observing the smallest of Nature's creations, we can gain insight into the mysterious workings of the universe at large, or alternatively, we can determine what we really believe by examining what we have in our lives. The problem for many of us is that we intuit that there is a Creator but have a hard time finding proof of its existence or feeling its presence in our daily lives. As a working hypothesis, "as above, so below; as below, so above" helps us to see that everything is a map of the One Life, which enables us to recognize and feel God's eternal presence, power, and wisdom everywhere.

Electricity is one such map. All matter, organic and inorganic, is made up of atoms, which contain electrons. The displacement of electrons from atoms generates electricity, which is a source of tremendous creative power. In addition, we notice that electrons always know what to do—whether they are flowing from one atom to the next to produce electricity, or they are orbiting a nucleus at a specific rate of vibration in a water molecule. And, because energy can neither be created nor destroyed, electrons are "eternal." While there is a clear correspondence between the scientific observation of electrons and our conception of Divinity, one intriguing question still remains. Did God make electrons, or are the electrons God?

A PAGE FROM LIFE

THE LAW OF THE LITTLE IS THE LAW OF THE BIG

Several years ago, I was offered a promotion at work that involved a lot more management responsibility. Once the euphoria of getting the job wore off, the panic started to set in—now I would have to deliver. I was an engineer who was lucky enough to have people skills— but what made me think that I could plan, budget, and delegate for a whole department?

I called my brother, who is two years younger than me, and told him what was going on. "I'm not trained in business. Sooner or later they're going to find out that I don't know what I'm doing." "But that's where you're wrong," he told me, "You do know what you're doing. Remember, the law of the little is the law of the big." He reminded me of how we had played office when we were kids. We would scribble notes on index cards and then file them in file boxes that our father brought home from his office. We used different color pencils for different jobs and wrote "documents" on a stack of pages with carbon paper sandwiched in between each sheet. We even named the company—The Hillside Corporation. My brother was usually the staff, and, you guessed it, I was usually the boss. I set up the game, decided what needed to be done, and gave him, and sometimes other kids on the block, their assignments. That management capability was in me when I was a nine, so what made me think I didn't have it now many years later?

Lily Tomlin once joked that if we'd all become what we said we wanted to be when we where kids, the country would be full of firemen, nurses, policemen, and ballerinas. We tend to ignore our childhood dreams because they are, well, childish. But, in many ways, our childhood behavior is the purest expression of who we are. How many times in our adult lives do we allow ourselves to dream or act out what's in our imagination in a totally uninhibited manner? If we can remember what we were like before we became aware of the outside expectations of us, then we might be better able to figure out what makes us happy today.

I am lucky that my brother has such an insightful memory from when he was seven years old. But I guess I shouldn't be surprised, after all, he was the best employee The Hillside Corporation ever had.

Karen

*If I'm to live a full life, I have to die
a thousand times each day. Every belief
I let go of is a death—the death of
an old identity that didn't serve.*
BYRON KATIE

Question 45

Are you dead to the world?

When we were children and everything seemed like a game, was that real? Walking would invariably turn into running, with the sole purpose of seeing how fast we could go. Eating, bathing, everything had play value. When we got a little older, wearing the right clothes or having the right hairstyle became more important than anything else. Was that the real world? What happened to the playground that absorbed our attention five years ago? Now we're adults and we're probably all thinking, "This is it, this is the real thing." But even in our adult lives, we're not exactly the same people we were five years ago. In fact, several years from now our current worries may seem as trivial to us as flinging peas across the room with a fork seems to us now.

We reinvent ourselves all the time, yet at each stage we're *certain* that what we experience right now, for better or for worse, is all that life has to offer us. But hindsight shows us that there are, and always were, other possibilities, we were just oblivious to them at the time. Just as it was necessary to let go of the playground to experience life as a teenager, and then to let go of the varsity letter jacket to become a young business professional, maybe we have to let part of our current selves die before we can be enlightened and see the bigger picture. Perhaps that's why it seems so frightening to *really* be hopeful or patient in the midst of a trying situation. The part of us that wants to respond with anger, worry, and fear is choking and gasping for breath to express itself. It's like we are dying. But just remember, we've survived this death many times—from infant to toddler, from teenager to adult—and hindsight has proven that each time we died, we really just started to live.

Part 4

The Pinnacle and Back, Again

The trick to effectively using our spiritual power is not to get too cocky. We may have tapped into our spiritual essence but the journey is just beginning. There's a lot more to be revealed, including how to return to the everyday world, get what we want, and serve life at the same time. It can be challenging to remember that we are spiritual beings when dealing with life's ups and downs, but we've got more knowledge and experience than ever before. Spirit has always been whispering in our ear. Now, if we listen, we can hear it.

*These bodies are perishable; but the
dwellers in these bodies are eternal,
indestructible, and impenetrable.*
THE BHAGAVAD-GITA

Question 46

How about letting go,
just a little?

By now you've gained a lot of knowledge about how
life works. You no longer fight everything, yet you get
what you want more often. You have moments of
peacefulness or focused concentration where the outside
world seems to fade away and you are left with a strong
sense that everything is as it should be. But wait. All of a
sudden you're thrust back into a situation that reminds
you of the old days. People are nasty, or something doesn't
go the way you planned and now you have to deal with
the repercussions. You thought all this would dissolve
with your new, enlightened attitude. But it's hard to
maintain that enlightened state 24/7. And if you did, the
world as you know it might fade away altogether and

who's really ready to let go of the whole world right now? If you can begin to let go just a little, then dealing with the day-to-day stuff can seem a whole lot easier. Don't take your earthly ties and material possessions so seriously—you wouldn't be on this path if those were your main goals anyway. Laugh at the idiots who used to make you crazy and give yourself a kick in the butt when maintaining appearances keeps you from doing what your heart desires. Have fun and remind yourself that everything will be OK even on those occasions when no one would mistake you for the Dalai Lama.

I think most people have
a natural instinct to rebel.
Elvis Presley

Question 47

Want something
to rebel against?

How about:

- your ego
- your pain
- judgment in any form
- prejudice in the name of love
- fear of death
- slavery
- selfishness

- martyrdom
- joylessness
- complacency
- anger
- hypocrisy
- envy
- rebellion.

In an ideal spiritual world we would all accept everything as is, and even the "flawed" would be perfect in its imperfection. But, as humans, we need something to push off of, sort of like a springboard, when we want to make changes in our lives. So why not choose to rebel against something worth rebelling against? Become a kick-ass spiritual revolutionary and stop blaming your bad luck, your boss, or your relatives. Dig for the deeper meaning.

A PAGE FROM LIFE

I FOUGHT THE LAW AND THE LAW WON

My Achilles' heel is anger and I've spent the better part of my adult life struggling against it—until recently. My story starts in 1963 with my earliest childhood memory—John F. Kennedy's assassination. I was three at the time, and my sister and I were playing with blocks. The television was on, something interrupted our kiddy show, and my mother raced into the room and burst into tears. I didn't understand what had happened but I knew two things: it wasn't good and it was beyond my control. In one fell swoop, I was thrown out of the Garden of Eden equipped with only a toddler's natural intuition. Pandora's box was open and, in a very real sense, I wasn't a baby anymore.

The next several years provided ample opportunities for me to experience and explore the idea of good and evil. Juxtaposed against the joys of childhood were the assassinations of Bobby Kennedy and Martin Luther

King, Jr., the horrors of the Vietnam War (remember the photo of the naked Vietnamese girl running down the street screaming or the pictures of the Buddhist monks setting themselves on fire?), the riots at the Democratic Convention, the Kent State massacre, and then, to top it all off, the Greek tragedy of Watergate. There are many in my generation who were seemingly unaffected by these events and for a while I considered them to be the lucky ones. But I had intelligent, politically active parents who, for better or worse, didn't shield us from the outside world. And, just like all parents throughout the course of history, they were sorting out their own issues while raising children—a difficult thing to do in the best of times.

I now see my childhood as perfect. But that's been a long time coming. Just like Adam and Eve, I wasn't happy at being tossed out of the Garden just because I had inadvertently eaten from the tree of good and evil. I became angry. Along with knowledge came insecurity, doubt, and stress over not being able to predict what was going to happen and not being able to make everything okay. There were times I wasn't even sure the world was going to be around for much longer. I was scared and I was stuck. I began looking for a way back to the Garden.

I found music, which strengthened my experience of beauty; literature, which developed my imagination; and philosophy, which encouraged my search for answers. I began to sense that there was something beyond good and evil that was the key to everything, the unifying principle, and the road home. But I couldn't shake my anger, which would rise up whenever I felt threatened, out of control, or deeply frustrated. I trudged on, ashamed of this powerful emotion, tired of being its slave, yet unable to become its master. I kept fighting it and it kept fighting me. It seemed the battle would never end. And then I got a gift. I realized that if I wanted peace, I had to stop fighting—and the first thing I had to stop fighting was anger itself.

Anger may be my Achilles' heel, but it is also my portal to enlightenment. Wasn't it anger that pushed me to look inward for the answers because I couldn't understand the strangeness and irrationality of the outside world? Wasn't it anger that turned me into a free thinker because I couldn't tolerate the religious/political dogma, which justified any amount of horror as long as it was done in the name of God or the government? Didn't anger at the way people mistreated each other help me to develop patience and compassion? Anger was my friend, not my enemy. It was my reaction to the emotion that was the problem. Anger was providing me with information about what was going on inside and helping me find out what I needed to do (or not to do) to make myself happy. Anger brought me back to the Garden and dragged me to the Tree of Life, which revealed the one great law: All is One. Once I stopped fighting and allowed anger to be at one with me, it lost its bite. I fought the law and the law won.

Tami

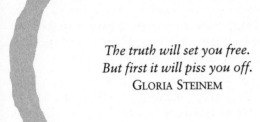

The truth will set you free.
But first it will piss you off.
GLORIA STEINEM

question 48

What's your secret?

Come on, you know you have one. Are you a secret smoker, closet eater, excessive drinker, drug addict? Do you have an alternative lifestyle that you hide from your job or family? Are you in too much debt or obsessed with managing your wealth? Do you feel unlovable, unworthy, unwell? Welcome to the human race. Nearly all of us has something we try to hide from even our closest friends and loved ones. We may think we are being clever by not revealing our self-destructiveness, our lack of understanding, or our hidden pain, but aren't we just black-mailing ourselves out of fear that we will be abandoned, or worse?

By demanding all our time and attention, these secrets drain our energy and prevent us from becoming enlightened to the underlying harmony and unity of existence. In truth, they only serve one purpose: to keep us enslaved to our egos. The ego is obsessed with external reality—the past, death, preserving the body, and outside approval. It can't see anything but it's own pain, so it spends its time trying to reveal and exploit other people's secrets so as not to feel completely alone. But the ego is the false self, the mask we wear because we haven't realized yet that we are eternal, spiritual beings made in the image and likeness of our Creator. It's time to let go of the secrets. The truth will set us free.

*We are part of one great Life, which knows
no failure, no loss of effort or strength, which
"mightily and sweetly ordering all things" bears
the worlds onwards to their goal.*
ANNIE BESANT

Question 49

Can you lay down your arms?

In life we are armed with primitive emotions that jump-start us when we need to take action. Fear gets us out of a dangerous situation; worry calls our attention to problems that need to be solved; and anger gives us the courage to stand up for ourselves. These gut reactions that make our adrenaline rush are weapons in our arsenal, which we rely on for earthly survival. But if they are not used properly, they cut us off from being happy. Too much anger perpetuates the idea that the world is a bad or hateful place, and too much worry can paralyze us with hopelessness. Yet, if we were to accept right now that everything is as it should be, there would be no cause to be angry or unhappy no matter what happened.

Ironically, it's only when you don't need these emotional weapons that you are qualified to use them. Only then can you be truly objective and understand that you are using them to achieve a goal, here and now, without letting their negative tone permeate your inner being. You can show anger when it is appropriate to correct someone's behavior without letting it eat away at you. But to get to this point you must lay down your arms and prove to yourself that you will be OK without them, that your life is not lessened when a driver cuts you off on the freeway or when your spouse complains, no matter how annoying it seems at the time. Once this is clear, you will be able to pick up your sword again, use it effectively, and know that no matter what happens, you can't lose.

A PAGE FROM LIFE

THE WORRY POLICE HAVE SUSPENDED MY LICENSE

After spending a weekend in Connecticut, I was driving back to the city on I-95, going along with the flow of traffic. My thoughts drifted from the events of the past two days to my to-do list for the coming week. I was hoping to hear back from the review committee to see if they'd accepted our proposal for a lecture by the Spiritual Chicks. There were so many things pending and I was worried that after months of a relatively flexible schedule, all of the engagements we had planned might end up being scheduled all at once. On top of that, if these events didn't coincide with the release of the book, we'd miss a good marketing opportunity.

As I sank deeper into this spiral of misaligned possibilities, nervous beyond belief that everything I was working for was about to happen but the timing might end up being all wrong, I heard a siren behind me. As the unmarked car came closer, I saw a flashing light in my rear view mirror, and then the PA system instructed me to pull over. A bit puzzled, I complied. I rolled down the window as the uniformed agent approached.

"What's the matter officer? I wasn't speeding. Is my taillight out or something?"

"No ma'am. Your car's just fine. It's your thinking that's the problem."

"My thinking?"

"Yes ma'am. You're fretting over things that haven't happened and may never happen. You're giving all your attention to the insignificant details when you're about to get the big break you've been waiting for. This is a flagrant misuse of your ability to reason."

"You pulled me over because I was worrying too much?" I asked.

"That's right," he replied as he wrote up the citation and handed it to me. I looked at the ticket. There was no fine involved, but I had to appear in court the next day.

As instructed, I went to the courthouse where the judge and the officer who had given me the ticket were waiting for me. I didn't get to plead my case, but there was nothing I could have thought to say anyway. I had done everything they accused me of doing. I hoped they'd be lenient. Then came the judge's verdict. "Worry," she told me, "is a serious tool meant to kick us into gear as a last resort. It's not something to be indulged in freely on a day-to-day basis. Until you learn to apply concern in proper proportion to the issue at hand, your worry privileges are suspended."

"What does that mean? I'm not allowed to worry?" I asked. "That's correct," replied the judge. "No worrying under any circumstances."

I left this surreal scene and tried to get back to my normal life. My head was starting to hurt from the stress of the courtroom drama. Or, maybe I was getting the flu—wouldn't that be great. I have so much work to do, I can't be sick right now—"Stop!" my inner voice chimed in. "You're worrying!" "But I'm just taking care of myself," I replied. "If you were taking care of yourself, you'd be doing something more constructive than sitting around wondering what terrible disease you might have," said the voice. "OK," I had to concede the voice had a point. Out of desperation, I closed my eyes for a five-minute micro-nap and the headache went away. Not too bad for my first worry-free day.

The next day things got a little tougher. Each time I heard about interest rates rising and stocks falling, or I had to do something that I knew someone else would not be happy about, I wanted to panic but I couldn't. When friends called to talk to me about their problems, I couldn't indulge them. That voice of reason loomed over me relentlessly. No matter how serious the situation was, I had to deal with it without worrying. To avoid worrying, I tried not to think too far ahead. There were times when I argued vehemently with the voice, "If you had only let me worry about this in advance, I wouldn't be at such a loss to deal with this problem now." But as I turned my attention to the present, focusing on what needed to be done at that particular moment, I began to relax. Gradually, I became less involved with the outcome of a particular situation and more interested in how I was handling things along the way. It was really quite peaceful.

I received a notice in the mail from the worry police saying that my license was reinstated. I stared at my license for a while wondering how I would use it. Why would they give something back to me that caused so much trouble in the first place? "Well," I thought, "I have gotten a little soft." In giving up worry cold turkey, I also gave up planning in advance and taking on situations that were too uncertain. Unfortunately, avoiding such challenges also meant I missed opportunities for growth. With this realization, the positive side of worry started to become apparent. Worry, in the form of proper planning and a healthy ability to identify problems before they become debilitating, gives us the courage to take on new experiences and offers the greatest possible hope for a beneficial outcome. So I decided that worry would be my warning signal—my call to action. Only now I knew that the required action was not the gnawing and fretting I had done before, but rather the calm focus that I had learned to apply during my brief period as an emotional outlaw.

Karen

We cannot change anything until we accept it.
Condemnation does not liberate, it oppresses.
CARL GUSTAV JUNG

Question 50

So you still don't believe we live in a perfect world?

It's not surprising. The idea that we live in a perfect world is the toughest metaphysical concept to understand, accept, and apply. But it's worth contemplating until we "get it," because it's the key to inner (and outer) peace. We have honed our ability to think critically to such a degree that it's become second nature (and the supposed mark of a high IQ) to find fault with everything we see, everyone we meet, and everything that happens. The irony of this approach to life is that we think we're "doing good" by thinking this way, after all it's the result of our desire to make things better or "perfect." But all we're really doing is looking for what's wrong, which enslaves us to the negative side of dualism. To be blunt, the quest for perfection by identifying, analyzing, and cataloguing everything that is "wrong" aligns us not with good but with evil, which is why external reality (on both the personal and the global levels) never seems to improve, no matter how hard we try.

As counterintuitive as it sounds, the solution is not to try make things better, but to see things more clearly. Everything that happens is perfect just the way it is. How can this be? In metaphysical terms, perfect doesn't mean "good;" it means "lawful." On the most essential level, everything is as it should be. It couldn't be any other way in an orderly, lawful universe that is governed by the One Life Principle. Once we understand and conform ourselves to the laws of the universe (cause and effect, for example), we align ourselves with the underlying perfection of the universe and are able to create anything we want. So, if we want peace in our lives and in the world, we have to stop finding fault and start looking for what's right.

Now, get out there and do it. We dare you.

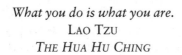

What you do is what you are.
LAO TZU
THE HUA HU CHING

Question 51

Are you ready to create the universe?

Hell no. Who wants that kind of responsibility? But the truth is, every thought, every emotion, every deeply rooted concept dictates the quality of our lives. So, in fact, each of us is creating our own universe already. The question is: are we interested in doing it consciously? If we want less anger in our lives, we need to start being more patient. If we want more love, we need to start loving more. If we want more money, we need to start appreciating the richness of what we have. Each time we make a decision to act a certain way and are conscious of the results, we become cognizant of our own creative power. We don't even have to make a "good" decision for this to be true. When we're in an ornery mood, something disagreeable will come along to satisfy our need to complain. It's not a reward/punishment scenario; it's just the way it is. So, are you ready to create your own universe? If you're like most of us, the answer varies from day to day. But that's OK, for the times when we're not up the task, the universe will make sure it happens anyway.

A PAGE FROM LIFE

IN HER HANDS SHE HOLDS LIFE ITSELF

Before I became a mother, I didn't really understand the creation process. Of course I knew about the birds and the bees, I just didn't get the big picture, or my role in it. Something inside me must have had a clue, however, because two weeks before I became pregnant, I felt compelled to go on a spiritual retreat at the Wisdom House in Litchfield, Connecticut. Wisdom House, a retreat and conference center, had been the Mother House for an order of Catholic nuns known as the Daughters of Wisdom. This order is devoted to Sophia, or Lady Wisdom—"the feminine face of God." Christianity is my cultural and religious heritage, but while I always had great appreciation for Jesus, I could never seem to muster up the same respect for the representatives of my own gender in the New Testament.

My introduction to Sophia shook me to my core. Having always considered myself rather rebellious and a free thinker, it shocked me to realize how strongly I had been influenced by the traditional Judeo-Christian idea of a masculine God. Even though I am a graduate of a women's college and a longstanding student of metaphysics, it took me until I was thirty-seven years old to come to grips with the idea that God had both masculine and feminine aspects, that both were equally important and powerful, and that creation—physical, mental and spiritual—could not happen without the interaction of the masculine with the feminine, the mind with the heart, the soul with the spirit. Before Sophia, my femaleness was a burden. I was only half a person. I was barren.

Who is Sophia? She is known by different names depending on the culture and tradition. She is called Nature, Shakti, Kali, Kwan Yin, Ishtar, the Shekinhah, the Blessed Virgin, the Holy Spirit, the World Soul. Some even say Jesus is an incarnation of Sophia. Just like God the Father, Sophia is everywhere, within and without. She is wisdom, sacred knowledge applied in everyday life, the bridge between heaven and earth. Sophia is the ancient, primordial, and universal Mother. She is the vessel for creation and the nurturer of that which she has birthed. She is raw and she is refined. She is the power and the glory.

I haven't been the same since I met Sophia. My mind stopped fighting my heart, and I conceived a new me. Almost simultaneously, I became pregnant and I knew I would have a girl. Nine months of growing ended in seventeen hours of labor, the most difficult and exhilarating experience of my life. I named my daughter Sophia.

Tami

We hold these truths to be self-evident, that all men are created equal, that they are endowed by their Creator with certain unalienable Rights, that among these are Life, Liberty, and the pursuit of Happiness.
THE DECLARATION OF INDEPENDENCE

Question 52

Can you mind your own business?

Have you ever done your best to help someone only to have him or her turn around and tell you to leave them alone? We can understand the rejection if our "help" doesn't lead to the desired result, but we're shocked by it when our efforts actually seem to improve the outcome. We might even wonder what the whole point of the spiritual journey is if we can't even use our experience to help other people move ahead. Welcome to earth. It's bizarre, but although some people complain bitterly about their circumstances, they don't necessarily want to change them. And as much as we feel sympathy for our fellow human beings and think that we do not judge them, when we assume that they want or need assistance, we walk the razor-thin line that separates constructive action from meddling.

No matter how well intended, when we interfere in the lives of others, we bind them to us, and not always in a good way. Offering unsolicited advice, even if it's accurate, imposes our expectations on other people and may very well interfere with their natural progression in life. If we piss them off, we burden them with anger; if we make them feel inadequate, we retard them with low esteem. We're not saying we have to pay lip service to every hair-brained scheme that comes our way, but if it doesn't affect us, and we haven't been asked for our opinion, we should probably restrain ourselves. And we must take care to evaluate what really affects us. Imposing our beliefs and demands on others who choose to live differently (especially under the guise of love, duty, or morality) selfishly enslaves them to us. But here's the kicker, they're not the only ones being enslaved—our own peace of mind is now tied to how well they meet our expectations. True freedom comes from feeling and using our power as spiritual beings; it does not depend on other people. So why would we burden ourselves by attaching our freedom to another who may seek to walk an entirely different path? It's a practical truth—if we want liberty, we've got to give it freely to others.

Compassion is the keen awareness of the interdependence of all things.
THOMAS MERTON

Question 53

What is compassion?

Well, it's not some namby-pamby term for letting people get away with murder, that's for sure. It's a state of mind, a perspective, a window on reality that comes from living in conformity with the One Life Principle. If indeed we are all One, then whatever one of us can do, we are all capable of doing—to one degree or another. Simply put, inside each of us is a potential artist, humanitarian, terrorist, or child molester. What we choose to express and manifest in this life depends on where we concentrate our energy, but our potential for both "positive" humanitarian actions and "negative" terrorist actions always exist. Compassion is the process of identifying how energy is being expressed at any given time and then aligning our actions with our highest potential as spiritual beings.

When we look into the eyes of our lover, we identify with love and automatically respond lovingly because it makes us feel good. When we witness a brutal act of destruction, we correctly identify hate as the energy behind the situation. As carnal beings, our automatic reaction may be to respond in kind, but as spiritual beings, we can choose to show compassion instead. If we desire everlasting life, freedom and justice, rather than death, restriction, and revenge, we respond out of love and let the chips fall where they may knowing that the energy that has created us and that sustains us will take care of the rest. Compassion is not about letting another person off the hook or about ignoring the consequences of hate crimes; in fact it's not about other people, places, situations, or things at all. It's about giving ourselves unrestricted access to the energy of the One Life in order to create what we want to experience. Compassion is the highest expression of spiritual power. When we love those who hate us, we identify with the creative energy of the universe, not with the circumstances we might face. The next time we're confronted with hateful people or conditions, we have to make a decision. Will we allow ourselves to create our own reality or will we let reality create us?

A PAGE FROM LIFE

IF YOU SEE THE BUDDHA
ON THE SUBWAY, PAY ATTENTION

I was on the subway yesterday afternoon and a homeless man came into the car and asked for money. He was particularly persistent—maybe because it was the last car of the train and he had nowhere else to go until the next stop. He was a white man, probably in his thirties, and except for a few rotten teeth, he didn't seem to be in bad shape physically. Normally I consider myself a sympathetic person, and although I don't always pull my wallet out in the middle of the subway (a deep-rooted protective mechanism going back to when I was in grade school), I give out money when it seems warranted. But, this guy really bugged me. He wasn't physically threatening, but I felt as if he was trying to bully a captive audience with his persistence. As I scanned the faces in the car, I noticed that I wasn't the only one who was disturbed. One man was carrying a large box containing a new TV. The look on his face was a conflicted mixture of guilt over his inadvertent display of opulence in front of this "have-not," and resentment toward anyone who asked for handouts when he had worked to pay for his new toy. Another woman looked tired and tried to avert her eyes from the homeless man as he paced back and forth in front of her. Others shifted in their seats and watched closely to see if anyone gave him money, as if they would follow suit. But no one gave him anything, not the dollar, the quarter, nor the thin dime he was bargaining for by the time the train reached the 14th Street Station.

With the protagonist gone, I began to consider why he had annoyed me so much. In all honesty, he did not meet my definition of helpless, he did not seem desperate enough. He was young, he was not physically disabled, in fact, he seemed as healthy as anyone else in the subway car. Why couldn't he work and be productive? He was not creating great music or art for which he was willing to starve. He was not even a member of some ethnic category—at least then my liberal tendencies could have rationalized that he was disadvantaged. Most notably, he was angry, and I have trouble with aggressive people. I did not stop to think that maybe he had something to be angry about. Maybe he had lost a loved one, or his parents were mean to him, or he just could not control his aggression. To me, anyone who projects that kind of energy is "well" enough to fend for themselves.

Should I have given him money to be in accordance with the One Life Principle? Not necessarily. His belligerence was real, and maybe his lesson in life is to work through his anger and not be rewarded for it. However, thoughts are powerful things, and I probably did not help him or myself by criticizing him because he didn't suit my image of a homeless person with a heart of gold. Let's face it, the homeless are hard people to love because they wear on their sleeve all those vulnerabilities we try to hide in ourselves. This man was so similar to me in age and ethnicity that his aggressive behavior triggered something in me that I could not ignore. To the extent that I resonated with his anger, I helped to keep it alive in both us. And that, I realized, is true evidence that we are all connected.

Karen

*Beyond thoughts and words, beyond
concepts and beliefs, beyond all that is
known and imagined, beyond the mind itself,
is Silence—the sacred hub of the universe,
the place where all differences dissolve,
where all conflicts cease, where all fear turns
to love, where all souls shine with the
same single flame of radiance.*
ROBERT RABBIN, A CALL FOR PEACE

Question 54

Are you having second thoughts?

The spiritual path is a way of life; it's not a vacation. Once we make the decision to seek the Truth, we must be prepared for periods of intense difficulty, for occasions when nothing seems to make sense, for times when we don't know what to think, much less what to do. We try to live up to our spiritual ideals, but our failures lead us to have second thoughts about our new perspective. Great! Let's celebrate! Second thoughts are exciting evidence that our old concepts are beginning to break down.

Before accepting the One Life Principle, the people, places, situations, and things in our lives might not have brought us spiritual bliss but they at least made sense to our egos. There were good people and bad people, right decisions and wrong decisions, happy times and sad times. We tried like hell to avoid pain and experience pleasure by rationalizing our flaws and blaming others for our unlucky breaks. But in the end, there was always someone or something that stood in the way of our peace and happiness. Then we found relief in a new set of beliefs that proclaimed that freedom was within reach. We didn't have to change the world all we had to do was change ourselves.

At the beginning of the journey, we had boundless energy and made quick progress. But, as we move closer to our core, our hidden beliefs that live in the shadows and secretly call the shots become exposed. They try to convince the ego to bring out the heavy artillery and initiate a take-no-prisoners fight to the finish. What recourse do we have during this dark night of the soul? Let the ego fight. And while it's distracted with its business, let's take every opportunity to go within, to go deeper than ever before, until we're in heaven.

*Everything that we see is a shadow cast
by that which we do not see.*
MARTIN LUTHER KING, JR.

question 55

Can you see through the illusion?

A good friend of the Spiritual Chicks tells a story about a child who smacked another kid in plain view of the entire playground and then denied it. "I didn't touch that kid," he declared flatly. His denial was so emphatic that even the adults who witnessed the event had momentary doubts about their own observations. But as the cry of the child who was slapped grew louder, they came back to their senses.

When we want to believe something, the mind takes every opportunity to assert the validity of the belief, even when we know on a deeper level that it's not true. It's all an illusion staged within our own minds, but we think of it as real. If we pay close attention to the contradictions of our so-called reality, however, the illusion starts to break down.

Why is it that some very intelligent people believe that taxes are an infringement on personal freedom, while others, equally as smart, believe they are a necessity and a duty? How can some people prosper during a recession while so many suffer financial loss? And, how can it be that public speaking, flying in a plane, or scaling a vertical mountain face are invigorating to some and horrifying to others?

Everything, and we mean everything, in life flows from the concepts we hold, but these concepts have no life in and of themselves. They need the spiritual life force—the creative principle—to bring them to life. The creative principle is what's real, the rest is smoke and mirrors, a hologram that can be arranged and rearranged as we change our concepts. When we understand this, the seemingly irreconcilable begins to make sense, and we start to deal directly with the creative process itself rather than our material reality. Our bodies and any physical conditions we might have, or other people and any annoying traits they might have, lose their sting when we see them as manifestations of the One Life. The next time you are confronted with cold, hard reality, remember that life isn't always what it seems. Behind the illusion is the power to change the world.

A PAGE FROM LIFE

THE LORD OF THE FLIES

Several months ago, a few flies decided to spend the winter in our apartment—I guess it was more convenient than Florida. My husband and I decided against using Raid and dedicated ourselves to a more gentle approach. We successfully trapped each of the insects in our dark bathroom where we left the window open for them to escape. All but one of the flies went toward the light, taking their chances in the cold January air. I dubbed the fly that wouldn't leave "Lord of the Flies" because of his steadfast determination to spend the rest of his days in our humble abode. But, as much as I admired his *moxie*, I can't say he was an unassuming houseguest. In fact, I'm convinced that he trained as a kamikaze pilot in a past life. Without warning or provocation, Lord Fly would buzz in my face a few times a day and wouldn't leave me alone until I yelled and swatted at him. For a while, I tried to sneak up on him to kill him with my hand (the gentle approach be damned)—but he always eluded me, even when his life began to near its end and he started to get slow and sluggish. Now I think that he was trying to communicate with me, but at the time, he just pissed me off. My two and one-half year-old daughter, on the other hand, would say goodbye to him when we left the house and greet him when we returned home. She accepted him as part of the family. The day we came home and our fly didn't greet us, I knew he had died. Strangely enough, once the buzzing in my ear stopped, I began to wonder if there might have been a deeper meaning to my encounters with the fly.

But why would the One Life try to get my attention through an insect? I'm not a nature girl. I don't like zoos or farms, hate to ride horses, and have never yearned to commune with chimpanzees. Come to think of it though, I do have a strong love for dogs, especially the family dogs from my childhood. I dream about our chocolate brown poodle who believed he was a German shepherd, and our first golden retriever who was as sweet as she was beautiful. Recently, I found out that our second golden retriever Cordelia, the last of our family dogs, had died. At first, I tried to put it in perspective—she was old and she'd had a good life. But lately, I've had to admit that I'm deeply upset about Cordelia's death. In fact, for a few days I felt like I was falling apart. About eleven years ago, my brothers, sister, and I bought Cordelia for my parents. She was an amazing dog. As gentle with older people as she was with newborn babies, she showed unconditional love toward everyone she met. To me, she represented the best of our family. Since we bought Cordelia, however, my relationship with my siblings has been disintegrating. Over the years, we have communicated less and less, and lately not much at all. Every now and then, I try, but my efforts seem to come across like the buzzings of an annoying insect that refuses to go away. Perhaps that's the reflection the One Life, through Lord Fly, was mirroring back to me. Rather than fighting the situation, which I clearly helped to create, I think I ought to take Cordelia's example to heart and practice unconditional love. Maybe then I can let go and head for the light like Lord Fly's more enlightened brethren.

Tami

Question 56

Can you take the "want" out?

Most of us don't realize the extent to which we're hypnotized to believe that our happiness and self-worth come from having an abundance of material things. And even those of us who do realize it, don't do much about it. Why? Because material things are like alcohol, cigarettes, and drugs, they provide short-term gratification; they temporarily make us feel high. But, as we all know, this high doesn't last long. Our new car gets a scratch as soon as it leaves the showroom; our computer is obsolete by the time we get it out of the box; a few extra pounds makes our trendy outfit look ridiculous. Then, we're left with that horrible, unquenchable feeling of wanting more—all over again. Hey, maybe we call ourselves consumers because the process of managing and trying to fulfill our many wants is all-consuming.

When we're constantly consumed by the desire for more, what we really feel is that we don't have enough, that our lives aren't good enough—that we aren't good enough. And that's dangerous territory. Life doesn't necessarily give us what we want, but it usually give us what we expect. When we focus on the negative side of the equation—on what's missing or what's lacking—we set ourselves up for disappointment and more lack on all levels. There's a simple solution, however. And as we've said before, it doesn't require giving up our toys or moving to a hut in the wilderness. Eliminate the negative by practicing gratitude. When we want a new computer, let's kiss the old one and thank it for serving us so well. By directing our energies from consuming—which is a passive approach to life based on lack—toward appreciating—which is an active approach based on the understanding that as spiritual beings we couldn't possibly need anything because we are everything—we find ourselves back in heaven where we belong.

> *Let me say, at the risk of seeming ridiculous, that the true revolutionary is guided by great feelings of love.*
> CHE GUEVARA

Question 57

Where are you going to put your power?

Let's be clear, the spiritual path is about power—heavy duty, revolutionary, life-altering power. When used constructively, this power can transform a barren desert into Shangri-La; it can create heaven on earth. But before we use it to build a New Jerusalem, we must use it to demolish all our rigid, oppressive, totalitarian ideas that separate us from our peaceful goals and make us miserable, fearful, intolerant, and mean. Yes, that's right. There is a war to be fought, but regardless of the jingoistic rhetoric that may surface at any given time around the world, the only war to end all wars is the one that's waged and won within. And as anyone who's tried to fight it knows, it ain't pretty. In metaphysical literature, this war is called the Battle of Armageddon because, in the end, the ego is annihilated, and the soul is freed.

What's so great about having a free soul if the struggle to unleash it results in the death of our cherished personalities? Because, to put it bluntly, our personalities, no matter how comfortable, charming, and attractive, are repositories for anger, hate, fear, jealousy, greed, and selfishness. They embody the illusion of "separateness" and keep us from knowing our true nature, which is love. Only by ridding ourselves of hate entirely can we know love, live lovingly, and fulfill our destinies as spiritual warriors. What is a spiritual warrior? Sitting Bull said that a warrior is a person who sacrifices him or herself for the good of others. We say that a spiritual warrior is someone who surrenders his or her ego to serve Life. Are you ready to fire the first shot? Get out there and look for the good and go about doing good, no matter what happens. Your ego will consider it an act of war. We guarantee it.

A PAGE FROM LIFE

PHONE SEX

Like many writers, I work from home, and much of my interaction with others is over the phone. I've written articles with Tami, pitched ideas to magazine editors, and strategized with our agent over the phone. I'm creating over the phone all the time, and this notion of tele-creation (what I like to call "phone sex") is not too hard to embrace when you have some mutual connection with the person on the other end of the wire (or wireless). But other times this mode of interaction is extremely frustrating—most notably when I have to "get it on" with technical support or customer service representatives. In considering how much time and emotional energy I spend on these seemingly trivial encounters, I began to wonder why they were so annoyingly unfulfilling.

Observation 1 - Based on a special offer for our apartment building, I decided to switch local phone providers. I had just quit my job and was feeling a bit powerless—a feeling that played itself out quite literally when our phone was disconnected as soon as we switched to the new provider. I struggled with incompetent customer service agents for five days until I finally got a hold of a manager who could fix the problem.

Observation 2 - In the process of renovating our newly purchased apartment, I discovered some problems with the original construction of the building. Already intimidated by the responsibility of overseeing our own electricians and carpenters while my husband was halfway around the world on a business trip, I now had to call the developer's contractor. I masked my panic by speaking with saccharine politeness to this man, who then proceeded to use my sympathetic ear to tell me about all of his problems. Feeling like he was walking all over me, I changed tactics and told him he could "deal with my problems or deal with my lawyer"—he promptly hung up on me.

Observation 3 - I once bought ten high quality coaxial cables, each of which came with a coupon for eight DVD rentals from a new Internet mail order company. When I called to claim the offer, the company had changed business models, was now charging by the month instead of by the movie, and offered me three free months as a replacement. I explained that my coupons were for eighty movies, and no one could realistically rent eighty movies in three months. However, having a soft spot for struggling e-businesses, I felt sorry for them and told the manager that I was flexible and asked her to propose what she thought was a fair equivalent. She called me back a day later and offered me six months of free service, plus a check for $90! I never would have expected that!

Each time I treated a service call as an act of co-creation and not an act of coercion, the experience and the outcome were much more favorable. On the other hand, as soon as the customer service representative became the object of my frustration, the process of creation went straight to hell. I must admit, it's easy to dehumanize a nameless, faceless person on the phone and blame them for my problem. But if I can't control myself in this situation, then I shouldn't be surprised when entire cultures dehumanize other cultures, resulting in destruction and war. Maybe that's human nature, and maybe the current mode of relating to each other at a distance offers an outlet for that pent-up need to do battle every now and then. But I believe that having things run smoothly in my day-to-day life ultimately alleviates that need to fight. Besides, I'm much happier being a creator than a victim—a fact I must remember the next time I have to "get it on" with a customer service representative.

Karen

> *For our vanity is such that we hold*
> *our own characters immutable,*
> *and we are slow to acknowledge that*
> *they have changed, even for the better.*
> E.M. FORSTER

Question 58

So now you think you're pretty special, huh?

One by one you shed your old beliefs that limit you in life. You seek knowledge in all that you do, and use faith when that knowledge is not there. You concentrate on hope, and use courage when your worry can't be contained. You're generous, considerate, and kind, and, in short, pretty damn wonderful. But, after conquering so much, you wonder why your mind is still so focused on everyday realities. You shout to the world "DON'T YOU SEE HOW WONDERFUL I AM? WHY HAS THE MEANING OF LIFE NOT YET BEEN FULLY REVEALED TO ME?"

Assuming all this is true—that you are the textbook model of enlightenment—then what is it that holds you back? Vanity, plain and simple. Your pride in your accomplishments is so excessive that you are still hanging around waiting for your applause. It's like admiring a great shot you made in tennis, only to lose the point on the return because your self-appreciation took your focus off of the game. It's difficult not to pat ourselves on the back when we've worked so hard, and self-confidence is a highly productive trait. But, the practical limitation of focusing on accolades is that these accolades then become our reward and we forego the opportunity to achieve greater accomplishments. And what happens if those around us don't see the value of our efforts—do we compromise our goals to gain approval? If we stay focused on contributing to Life, then true wisdom becomes our reward. Wisdom is what allows us to create what we choose in our own lives. Wisdom makes us divinely indifferent to the musings of others and at the same time, deeply connects us to all that is.

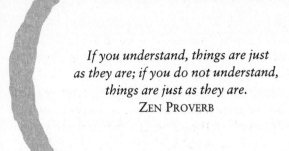

> *If you understand, things are just*
> *as they are; if you do not understand,*
> *things are just as they are.*
> ZEN PROVERB

Question 59

Who do you think you are?

Whether we're religious or not, most of us wonder who we are in relation to the mysterious energy or power that creates the universe. The remarkable thing is that there are many differing views on who we are, yet all who hold a particular view seem to feel it is validated by personal experience. Apparently, Life/Nature/Energy/God is exactly what we think it is. If we think it has no rhyme or reason, then we see chaos around us. If we think it is lawful, orderly, and impartial, then we see patterns and systems. If we think it's judgmental and wrathful, then we suffer our consequences. But if we think Life is a limitless creative principle, then we are able to understand how all of the above can be true at the same time. This is the most compelling reason to align ourselves with the One Life Principle—it just makes sense.

Some of us accept this intellectually, but we still go around criticizing many aspects of life as if they somehow are not expressions of the One. We cry at funerals instead of rejoicing in the knowledge that our loved one is safe and that their true essence cannot die. We panic during times of great confusion, instead of remaining calm because we know that everything has a purpose in life even if we don't see it yet. If we want to move beyond life's limitations, we have to first see Life as limitless, and this means assuming that anything we see as "bad" is merely something we don't fully understand. It's only by making this assumption that we set ourselves up to understand. So, if you think you are part of the divine essence that unites us all, and you want to explore the full potential of that essence, try aligning yourself with the grandest notion of them all— that there's only One Life, and you're it!

A PAGE FROM LIFE

DANCING WITH DIVINITY

To me, the most mind bending and inescapable implication of the One Life Principle is that on the deepest and most "real" level, I don't exist as a separate individual and neither do you. OK, fine, but, if I accept the underlying premise that God/One Life/Divinity is all-present, all-powerful, and all-knowing, then who exactly am I? And, why am I here?

If God is everywhere and there isn't any place where God is not, then it stands to reason that I am God and so is everyone else—the saints and the sinners, the good, the bad, and the ugly. It's hard to stomach, but serial killers, child molesters, and Adolph Hitler are also God—and so is Satan. And, since God is absolutely everywhere, then tables and chairs (and crystals and marijuana) are also God. Well, that explains how some people can have meaningful encounters with rocks and why I felt so spiritual my senior year in college, but it's still weird, isn't it? Well, not if God is an impersonal force (*may the force be with you*), an underlying energy, an organizing principle, and not a bearded guy in the sky. Why even Einstein's famous equation $e=mc^2$ implies that matter (you, me, tables, crystals) and energy (the scientific equivalent of God) are interrelated, maybe even the same thing once you factor in that pesky speed of light[2]. OK, but God is not just everywhere, God is also all-powerful and all-knowing. Does that imply that a table is as powerful as a mother lion protecting her cubs or as intelligent as a five-time winner on *Jeopardy*? Must be, at least inherently, but the table can't express itself in the same way as a mother lion or a *Jeopardy* champion. Neither can an impersonal force, come to think of it. Oh, I get it. God simply uses the diversity of matter to experience and express itself. So, when all is said and done, I'm simply a human expression of God with only one job to do—experience and express myself. In other words, I'm here to dance with Divinity. On the days I lead the dance, God repeats my steps and gets to experience humanity. But, on the days I remember my true identity, God leads the dance and I get to travel at the speed of light[2] and experience Divinity. Either way, it's a hell of a tango.

Tami

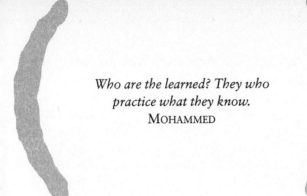

*Who are the learned? They who
practice what they know.*
MOHAMMED

Question 60

Can you walk the path of right action?

All the spiritual insights in the universe can't save us from the fact that we have to put these insights to use in our everyday lives to reap the benefits. After casting aside the myths and limiting ideas that held us down, we have to go back to the world in which they were created and continue on. It may sound like a drag, but what good is all that spiritual knowledge if we can't use it to better our lives? It's wisdom we're after, and wisdom only comes through experience. But what is it that we're trying to experience? Suffering or deprivation in the name of the higher self? No, although it may seem that way until we get the hang of it. What we're trying to experience is ourselves, plain and simple. Not the self that was defined by the ego, the self that knows that it's part of the One Great Life.

Our duty in life—our work to perform—is to express who we are in every moment. On the good days, we remember that we're part of the One, and express this notion in all that we do as individuals. This is right action. On the more frustrating days, we see ourselves as separate entities and act accordingly. But don't despair, this is right action too, because it's a true expression of who we are in that moment. And when suffering the consequences of being separate from our source becomes more than we can bear, we will find our way back to the One. So you see, if you are true to yourself, you can't go wrong in the end.

Nature relies on each of us to express a unique talent or purpose that can only come through our form, so it's divinely ordained that we be ourselves. With this as our mission, whatever it is that gives us the most pleasure or satisfaction is right action in that moment. If what gives us pleasure ultimately causes pain for ourselves or anyone else, this pain motivates us to redefine ourselves, until we find that, quite naturally, our pleasure is the pleasure of the One. In that instance of harmonizing with the divine, we find enlightenment— we find ourselves.